As You Like It

ARDEN STUDENT SKILLS: LANGUAGE AND WRITING

Series Editor
Dympna Callaghan, Syracuse University

Published Titles
Antony and Cleopatra, Virginia Mason Vaughan
Hamlet, Dympna Callaghan
King Lear, Jean E. Howard
King Richard III, Rebecca Lemon
Macbeth, Emma Smith
A Midsummer Night's Dream, R. S. White
Much Ado about Nothing, Indira Ghose
Othello, Laurie Maguire
Romeo and Juliet, Catherine Belsey
The Tempest, Brinda Charry
Twelfth Night, Frances E. Dolan

Forthcoming Titles
The Winter's Tale, Mario DiGangi

As You Like It

Language and Writing

ABIGAIL ROKISON-WOODALL

THE ARDEN SHAKESPEARE
LONDON • NEW YORK • OXFORD • NEW DELHI • SYDNEY

THE ARDEN SHAKESPEARE
Bloomsbury Publishing Plc
50 Bedford Square, London, WC1B 3DP, UK
1385 Broadway, New York, NY 10018, USA
29 Earlsfort Terrace, Dublin 2, Ireland

BLOOMSBURY, THE ARDEN SHAKESPEARE and the Arden Shakespeare
logo are trademarks of Bloomsbury Publishing Plc

First published in Great Britain 2021

Copyright © Abigail Rokison-Woodall, 2021

Abigail Rokison-Woodall has asserted her right under the Copyright, Designs and Patents Act, 1988, to be identified as author of this work.

For legal purposes the Acknowledgements on p.vii constitute an extension of this copyright page.

Cover image: *As You Like It,* Act II Scene VII (© Folger Shakespeare Library)

All rights reserved. No part of this publication may be reproduced or transmitted in any form or by any means, electronic or mechanical, including photocopying, recording, or any information storage or retrieval system, without prior permission in writing from the publishers.

Bloomsbury Publishing Plc does not have any control over, or responsibility for, any third-party websites referred to or in this book. All internet addresses given in this book were correct at the time of going to press. The author and publisher regret any inconvenience caused if addresses have changed or sites have ceased to exist, but can accept no responsibility for any such changes.

A catalogue record for this book is available from the British Library.

Library of Congress Cataloging-in-Publication Data
Names: Rokison-Woodall, Abigail, 1975– author.
Title: As you like it : language and writing / Abigail Rokison-Woodall.
Description: London ; New York : The Arden Shakespeare, 2021. | Series: Arden student skills: language and writing | Includes bibliographical references and index.
Identifiers: LCCN 2020052051 (print) | LCCN 2020052052 (ebook)
ISBN 9781350120419 (hardback) | ISBN 9781350120433(ebook) | ISBN 9781350120440(epub)
Subjects: LCSH: Shakespeare, William, 1564-1616. As you like it.
Classification: LCC PR2803 (ebook) | LCC PR2803 .R65 2021 (print) | DDC 822.3/3—dc23
LC record available at https://lccn.loc.gov/2020052051

ISBN: HB: 978-1-3501-2042-6
PB: 978-1-3501-2041-9
ePDF: 978-1-3501-2043-3
eBook: 978-1-3501-2044-0

Series: Arden Student Skills: Language and Writing

Typeset by RefineCatch Limited, Bungay, Suffolk

To find out more about our authors and books visit www.bloomsbury.com and sign up for our newsletters.

CONTENTS

Abbreviations vii

Introduction 1
    Dating the play 2
    Printing the play 3
    The first folio and its copy 4
    The Elizabethan theatre 5
    Blank verse drama 12
    The conventions of prose 12
    A classical education 14
    Shakespeare's biblical language 21

1 Language in Context 25
    Genre 25
    Festive comedy 31
    Pastoral 32
    Source and setting 36
    Characters 44
    Metatheatre 53
    Masque 54

2 Language: Forms and Uses 59
    Verse and prose 59
    Personal pronouns 84
    Asides and soliloquies 88
    Rhetoric 90

3 Language Over Time 99
Issues of interpretation 99
Contemporary references, changing meanings and archaic language 107
Interpretation of language on the modern stage 116
As You Like It on film: where pictures do the work 120

4 Performing the Language 125
Performing metre 125
Performing rhetoric 141
Performing 'you' and 'thou' 150

Bibliography 155

ABBREVIATIONS

RSC   Royal Shakespeare Company
NT   National Theatre
OED   Oxford English Dictionary
F1   Folio 1
Ham. *Hamlet*
1H4   *King Henry IV, Part 1*

Introduction

At first glance, the play of *As You Like It* does not seem particularly controversial or seditious. There is little violence, no bloody deaths of the type found in most of Shakespeare's tragedies and no explicit sexual content. Indeed, a censor akin to those on a modern film classification board might be forgiven for considering the play universally suitable for a general audience. And yet, there is something mysterious about the early history of *As You Like It* which seems to suggest that it was deemed unsuitable for publication in the early 1600s. The first reference to the play appears on 4 August 1600, in what is known as a staying order in the Stationers' register. A staying order is an expression of intent to publish a play which prevents anyone else from printing it, and this particular order was for four plays – all owned by the theatre company of which Shakespeare was a member, The Lord Chamberlain's Men – *Henry V, Much Ado About Nothing,* as well as a play by Shakespeare's contemporary Ben Jonson's *Every Man in His Humour* and *As You Like It*.

      4 Augusti
As yo^w like yt: / a booke
Henry the ffift: / a booke
Euery man in his Humo^r. / a booke   to be staied
The cōmedie of muche
A doo about nothinge. / a booke

However, unlike the other three plays, which were printed shortly after being 'staied', *As You Like It* had to wait another twenty years to appear in print. We don't know why the play wasn't printed in

1600, but one possible explanation is that the censor didn't approve of the satirical character of Jaques whose name could be pronounced 'Jakes', slang for lavatory. It is, however, not merely the mild toilet humour that is likely to have offended the censor, but the connection between the word 'Jakes' and the political landscape of the early 1600s. In 1596, Sir John Harington, godson to Elizabeth I, had published a scatological satire about his invention of the water closet, entitled *The Metamorphosis of Ajax* (A Jaks/A Jakes). Harington was out of favour with the queen because of his associations with the Earl of Essex. The second Earl of Essex, Robert Devereux, had been a particular favourite of Queen Elizabeth I. However, in September 1599, following a failed campaign in Ireland, he returned to England without permission from the queen and was put under house arrest. In 1601 he mounted an attempted rebellion against Elizabeth and was executed for treason. It may be that a play that appeared to have links to Harington was deemed unpublishable.

Dating the play

Although the play was not published until 1623, the reference in the Stationers' register helps us in dating the play's composition. *As You Like It* must have been written by mid 1600. This reference provides us with the latest date at which the play could have been written. To narrow down the window of composition, we must also establish the earliest possible date as which the play could have come into existence. This is usefully provided in the text of *As You Like It* itself, in a line spoken by the shepherdess Phoebe:

> Dead shepherd, now I find thy saw of might:
> 'Whoever loved that loved not at first sight.'
>
> (3.5.82–3)[1]

A 'saw' is a wise saying, and this one comes from Christopher Marlowe's poem *Hero and Leander*, which, whilst mostly written in around 1593, was not published until 1598. Although a number of critics have argued that Shakespeare may have had access to Marlowe's

---

[1] The system for citing from the plays has been shortened to omit the words 'act' and 'scene'. The act number precedes the scene number, separated by a full point.

poem in manuscript, there would have been little point in him inserting a direct quotation of this kind if it were not to be recognized by at least some of the audience as a tribute to his dead friend. So – the play seems to have been written between 1598 and 1600.

The question of where the play was first performed also has some bearing on its dating. Some have argued that Jaques' line 'All the World's a Stage' (2.7.140) is a direct reference to the Globe Theatre, which opened in May 1599, and suggests that *As You Like It* was one of the first plays to be performed in the new space in mid to late 1599. Whilst the often quoted assertion that the Globe had a motto, *Totus mundus agit histrionem* (The whole world moves the actor; often mis-translated as 'All the world's a stage') has now largely been discredited, as Gabriel Egan asserts, there is a tantalizingly suggestive correspondence between the name of the theatre, as something referencing 'the microcosmic correspondence of the world of drama and the world of everyday life' (2001: 166) and the words that begin Jaques' speech on this theme.

Juliet Dusinberre uses another of the play's lines to suggest a slightly earlier date of February 1599 for the play's first performance. Citing Touchstone's quip about the 'certain knight that swore by his honour they were good pancakes, and swore by his honour the mustard was naught' (the mustard was no good), Dusinberre suggests that the play may have been first performed at Richmond Palace on Shrove Tuesday (February) 1599 (2006: 40). Shrove Tuesday is a Christian feast day that takes place immediately before the start of Lent. It is traditional to eat pancakes (and other food made with butter and eggs) on this day, since these foods were usually given up during the Lenten period. Whichever of these original performance locations is correct, the cumulative evidence seems to date the play to between early 1599 and spring 1600. The dating of the play is important, as we will see, for discussions about the use of verse and prose, the nature of the Fool, the depiction of Rosalind and Celia, and the original staging conditions.

Printing the play

As You Like It is one of eighteen plays by Shakespeare that appears for the first time in 1623 in the collection of Shakespeare's work entitled *Mr. William Shakespeares Comedies, Histories, & Tragedies.*

This publication was put together by Shakespeare's friends and colleagues John Hemminges and Henry Condell and is referred to as the First Folio of Shakespeare's work (a folio being a large book of around 15 inches (38 centimetres) in height, a format usually reserved for prestigious works by leading theologians, historians and philosophers). The First Folio contained thirty-six of the plays, eighteen of which had been printed before in quarto form. Although the title page of the Folio claims that these plays are 'Published according to the True Original Copies', the copy texts (the documents from which the printers put together the play texts) vary in origin – from quarto texts (small individual copies of the plays published during Shakespeare's lifetime), manuscripts derived from authorial copy (that is the script in Shakespeare's own handwriting, which does not survive), scribal copy (a clean copy of the play text made by a scribe) and prompt books (the copy of the play put together for use in the theatre).

The first folio and its copy

As You Like It seems to have been printed from a fairly clean, unproblematic manuscript. This does not point towards 'foul papers' (authorial draft), from which one might expect inconsistent speech prefixes, 'Shakespearean' spellings and sparse punctuation. However, neither does the nature of the text suggest a marked-up prompt copy. Something not easily apparent to those working from modern editions of the play is that the manuscript from which the play was printed appears to have been neatly divided into acts and scenes. This is something that modern editors do with all Shakespeare's plays, splitting them into five acts each containing a number of scenes. However, this is not a consistent feature of the plays as printed in the early quartos and Folio, and it is not something that would have been necessary for a prompt book, being a literary rather than a theatrical convention. The manuscript behind the Folio thus appears to be some sort of literary transcript of either authorial or playhouse copy. Given the lack of a quarto edition, there are very few textual variants for the reader or actor to take into account, the few that exist being minor 'corrections' made to the second or third Folios (typically referred to by critics as F2 and F3). Further corrections have been made by subsequent editors and may appear in modern editions of the play.

The Elizabethan theatre

In order to fully understand a play like *As You Like It,* one need to understand the theatrical conventions of the period in which it was written, and thus the theatres for which it was composed. As has been discussed, there is some disagreement as to where the play was originally performed. There is no record of a public performance until 1740. Martin Wiggins places the play's first performance in the Globe Theatre on Bankside (2014: 212) in 1600, whilst Juliet Dusinberre suggests that it may have been one of the interludes or plays presented before the queen at Richmond Palace on 20 February 1599, later gracing the Globe Stage as part of its opening season (2006: 36–46). There is also some evidence that performances may also have taken place at the Blackfriars Theatre, the indoor playhouse acquired by the King's Men (formerly the Lord Chamberlain's Men) in 1608. The play appears in a list of 108 plays, twenty-one by Shakespeare, which had been 'formerly acted at the Blackfriars' and were now permitted to be performed by 'his Majesties Servants' (The King's Company) at 'The New Theatre' (The Theatre Royal) (Dusinberre, 2006: 43). Although we have no records of early performances of the play, we can piece together certain evidence that might tell us something about what those performances must have been like – the nature of the theatres in which they took place, the staging conventions associated with these theatres, and the actors that might have been in them.

The Globe Theatre (and the other amphitheatres of the Early Modern period) had certain features which would have influenced the staging, and indeed the composition of the plays – a thrust stage extending out into an auditorium with multiple sides (almost circular in appearance); three entrances to the stage – a door on either side of the stage and a central opening (sometimes referred to as a discovery space); two pillars supporting the 'heavens', a painted covering extending over most of the playing space; a trap door in the floor that appears to have been mechanized; and a gallery over the stage that was used for staging certain scenes. There would have been a number of musicians, playing either from within the tiring house (the backstage area immediate behind the stage) or on the balcony (the galleried area above the back of the stage). *As You Like It* does not make obvious use of the different levels of the stage – there are no scenes that appear to occur 'aloft' (on the balcony), or 'within' (in the discovery space) and none that seem to demand the use of the trap door in the stage. Egan states that of the plays written for the Globe 'none calls for a character to "fly"', concluding that it is 'unlikely that the Globe had a flight machine when it was first built' (2001: 166). The only conceivable use of the heavens trap (another trap door in the canopy that overhung the stage) in *As You Like It* might be for the appearance of the god Hymen in 5.4, since it was customary for gods and goddesses to 'descend' from the 'heavens'. However, whilst some productions choose to present Hymen, at face value, as the visible manifestation of a god (a 'theophany'), this is a difficult moment in a play that is otherwise devoid of the supernatural, and it has become traditional for Corin, the shepherd, or one of the other characters to 'perform' the part of Hymen.

The thrust stage configuration of a playhouse like the Globe would have made the use of any sizeable pieces of scenery difficult due to the obstruction of sight lines. Without recourse to blackouts (the ability to make the stage go dark by turning out all the lights) or a front curtain (as might be found in a proscenium arch, front-on theatre), scene changes out of view of the audience were also not possible, meaning that a transition such as that between 1.3 (the court) and 2.1 (the forest) in *As You Like It*, would have had to be effected reasonably swiftly and simply. It has long been argued that the Globe employed minimal scenery and limited properties. However, an inventory for a list of properties owned by the Lord Admiral's Men at the Rose Theatre (discovered and published by Edmond Malone, but now lost), indicates that 'the Elizabethan stage was not as bare as has sometimes been argued' (Rutter, 1984: 134). There are references to a rock, a cage, a tomb, coffins, 'stairs for Phaeton', and even 'the city of Rome' (probably a painted backdrop). There are also listings for numerous trees – a bay tree, a tree with dead limbs, Tantalus's tree and a tree of golden apples. The only sizeable items of scenery implied by the text of *As You Like It* are trees, on which Orlando can hang his verse in 3.2. It is plausible that the pillars might have been put into service as trees, as in recent productions at Shakespeare's Globe theatre, although eminent Shakespearean scholar E. K. Chambers, in his seminal four volume work on the Elizabethan stage, suggests in a footnote that trees, such as those recorded in the inventory of the Admiral's Men, were 'most likely' put into position by the use of the stage trap (1923: 107).

Bernard Beckerman asserts that of the 345 scenes in Shakespeare plays written for the Globe, more than 200 are unlocated, meaning that no specific location is indicated or indeed required (1962: 235). When location is important to a scene Shakespeare usually has characters vocalize it, language rather than scenery doing the work of establishing place. In *As You Like It,* for example, we know that 1.1 takes place in Oliver's orchard, because Orlando tells us – 'here in your orchard' (1.1.40); when we move to the forest in 2.1, this is conveyed in the first few lines of the scene – 'Are not these woods / More free from peril than the envious court?' (2.1.3–4); and when we return to the forest in 2.4 Rosalind states clearly 'Well, this is the Forest of Arden' (2.4.13). With plays in the Elizabethan playhouse being performed in the afternoon, in broad daylight, with no recourse to lighting effects, time of day is also largely defined by characters – 'Good morrow to your worship' (1.1.91); 'is't not past two o'clock?' (4.3.1), 'Good ev'n' (5.1.14).

Another key area of Elizabethan staging that merits further discussion in understanding the plays is that of the relationship between what Robert Weimann terms 'representation' and 'presentation' (1978, *passim*). Elizabethan ideas about naturalism or realism differed significantly from those of the modern theatre. One of the most obvious features that would have required a degree of suspension of disbelief was the portrayal of female roles by boy actors. There is some debate over the extent to which boy actors attempted to conceal their maleness. As Michael Shapiro argues, 'We may never know exactly how much distance play-boys put between themselves and their female characters: they may have merely indicated these roles rather than representing women more or less illusionistically' (1994: 37). An account by an audience member of a performance of *Othello* by the King's Men in Oxford in 1610 gives some indication that, in this instance at least, the boy player and the female character merged in the spectator's mind, the pronoun 'she' seeming to refer simultaneously to the female character and the boy performing the role:

> But indeed Desdemona, killed by her husband, although she always acted the matter very well, in her death moved us still more greatly.
>
> (qtd. Gurr, 1992: 226)

Nevertheless, as Tiffany Stern suggests, 'No doubt one reason why girls are so frequently dressed as boys in Shakespearean dramas' – as Rosalind is in *As You Like It* – 'is that it is easier for a boy to play a boy than a girl' (2004: 105–6).

As Stephen Purcell asserts, 'If we use the term [metatheatre] in its broadest sense – to describe any theater that in some way draws attention to its own artifice – it becomes evident that early modern drama is always "metatheatrical" to some extent' (2018: 19). *As You Like It* is one of the most metatheatrical of Shakespeare's plays, partly because it is a play concerned with disguise in which characters are consistently 'performing', and hence drawing attention to their own fictive status and partly because it is consistently made up of scenes in which characters observe one another, acting as a sort of on stage audience, and hence drawing attention to the process of watching theatre. We will examine the language of metatheatre in the play in more detail in Chapter 1, whilst in Chapter 2 we will explore the metatheatrical implications of soliloquies (speeches in which a character, alone on stage, expresses their feelings aloud) and asides (a remark not intended to be heard by everyone on stage, spoken either to another character or to the audience), both features of the Elizabethan theatre that draw attention to its unreality.

There are numerous points in Shakespeare's plays where characters, alone on stage, speak their thoughts or feelings aloud. These moments are often referred to, anachronistically, as the 'breaking of the fourth wall' (we cannot break down a wall that has not yet been built). Although two recent studies of soliloquies in Shakespeare have argued for self-address rather than direct audience address as the most frequently mode of delivery for soliloquies (Nordlund, 2017; Hirsch, 2003), I tend towards the opinion, widely expressed by critics and practitioners, that such moments are frequently indicative of direct address to the audience. Bridget Escolme argues that 'talking to the audience' was a 'key convention of Shakespeare's theatre' (2004: 5) and Weimann develops the term '*platea*' to denote the liminal space between actor and audience, from which the former can directly address the latter (1978).

Certainly directors and actors working at the new Shakespeare's Globe theatre have tended to conclude that audience address is inevitable in this space:

> An actor cannot go out onto that stage and give a soliloquy without speaking directly to the audience. It would be perverse: they are clearly in the same place as the actor.
>
> (Tim Carroll, 2008: 40)

One of the reasons for debates over the nature of asides on the Elizabethan stage is that the term 'aside' is rarely found in the Shakespearean canon. Nevertheless, there are a large number of unmarked but obvious asides in the plays. Asides can be delivered to an audience or to another character on stage, but they function in similar ways – allowing a character to comment privately on the action, unheard by one or more characters on stage, and thus reveal their true feelings about something. As Alan Dessen explains, one of the main issues with asides has been an assumption that a degree of realism is necessary for their delivery; that 'to deliver an aside a Richard III or Hamlet or Othello must be distanced from the other figures on stage' (1984: 9). However, Elizabethan actors may not have been concerned with creating the illusion of realism and may simply have signalled an aside through body language or tone of voice. For Dessen, our understanding of elements such as 'soliloquies, asides, disguises, eavesdropping scenes' depends on a shared 'working definition of "theatrical convention"' (1984: 9–10), a definition that accepts that what we might find palatable in a post-Stanislavskian theatrical context (where realism in has become a norm in Western theatre) may not equate to what Elizabethan or Jacobean audiences expected or accepted. As one might expect, different editions annotate asides in different ways. The major scholarly editions of *As You Like It* are not in agreement about the location of asides in the play. Whilst this may not seem particularly significant for a reader, it can make a great difference to actors and their relationships with audiences.

Dessen's categories of 'eavesdropping scenes' and 'disguise' are both particularly pertinent to *As You Like It*, and, as discussed above, inherently metatheatrical. Hugh Macrae Richmond describes 'overhearings' as 'a major device in Shakespeare', reflecting 'the curious fitness of the permanent format of broad and deep

Elizabethan stages' (2002: 325). What Richmond invokes is the possibility of characters lurking on the outer edge of the stage or hiding behind a pillar, seen by the audience, but not, in an accepted convention, by the other characters onstage. There are a number of such instances in *As You Like It*:

- Adam, instructed by Orlando to 'Go apart' to overhear his conversation with his brother Oliver (1.1.25).
- Duke Frederick standing aside: 'I'll not be by', whilst Rosalind and Celia attempt to persuade Orlando from fighting (1.2.156).
- Rosalind, Celia and Touchstone observing the conversation between Corin and Silvius (2.4).
- Rosalind and Touchstone standing 'aside' to hear Celia read one of Orlando's poems (3.2.120–1).
- Celia and Rosalind observing the conversation between Orlando and Jaques: 'Slink by and note him' (3.2.245).
- Jaques overhearing the dialogue between Touchstone and Audrey (3.3).
- Rosalind, Celia and Corin observing Phoebe and Silvius (3.5).

In each of these cases it seems as important for the audience to be able to observe the spectators as those being watched, creating a split-screen effect which is familiar to cinema viewers, but more difficult to achieve on stage, without the construction of some sort of structure for the overhearers to lurk behind.

Disguise is, as discussed, another common motif of Early Modern drama about which audiences are clearly expected to suspend disbelief. In *As You Like It* we are supposed to accept, for example, that Rosalind's father does not recognize his own daughter simply because she is wearing men's clothes. Of course, cross-gendered disguise would have had different implications for a Renaissance audience than for a modern one. As Peter Hyland asserts, 'Modern performances of transvestite disguise roles are inevitably misleading if we think of them as a replication of what the original audience might have seen' (2011: 3). A boy actor playing a character disguised as a boy must have seemed quite convincing, whereas a female actor, even if given a short hairstyle and some trousers, is unlikely to seem 'anything other than a woman dressed as a man' (Hyland, 2011: 3). Nevertheless, Hyland describes all devices of disguise as 'in essence metatheatrical' since 'what the disguiser does is what the stage player does: he or she dresses up and pretends to be someone else' (2011: 91).

I return now to the possibility suggested by Dusinberre, that *As You Like It* may have been written initially, not for the public stage, but for the court. In terms of the dramaturgical features of the play, these are not likely to have been greatly affected by an early performance at court. As John H. Astington suggests, it seems likely that 'by 1600 the arrangement and layout of stages and tiring houses at court would have been made to suit prevailing professional practice', making the transition from court to public theatre reasonably easy for the professional players (1999: 110). Dusinberre suggests that if *As You Like It* was performed in the Great Hall at Richmond it was probably staged with an audience 'on three sides and the royal party on the dais', the performers 'in the space at the center of the Great Hall and on the dais just in front of the queen's dining table' and the musicians 'at the "lower" end of the hall in the gallery' (2003b: 393). Much like in the outdoor playhouses, the actors would thus have been surrounded by their audience (within close proximity to many), in the same light as the spectators, and would have had little recourse to fixed scenery, which would have obscured sight lines. With no scenes taking place aloft or within, or demanding the use of a trap door, *As You Like It* would have been reasonably easy to stage in this locale. It is thus less the space, and more the audience which Dusinberre suggests it likely to have impacted on the play and its composition. She draws attention to 'the many characteristics which might relate the play to the tastes of the Court and private theatres rather than to those of the public theatre audience' (2006: 43), the pastoral setting, the quantity of music, the wedding masque and the witty wordplay and satire (2003b: 374). The evidence on which Dusinberre makes her assertions, whilst intriguing, is far from conclusive, and irrespective of whether the play was first performed in a court setting, it would, undoubtedly also have been intended for the public playhouses and a wider audience. One of the most significant implications for Dusinberre's argument relates not to the location of the play's premiere, but to the date and the impact that this would have had on the casting of the clown.

Blank verse drama

When we consider some of the presentational features of Shakespeare's plays, one of the main elements of artificiality is arguably that of blank verse, the principal medium of most of the plays. Blank verse is essentially made up of unrhymed lines of iambic pentameter: five feet, each one made up of an unstressed syllable followed by a stressed syllable, and annotated u/ u/ u/ u/ u/. Shakespeare inherited his dramatic blank verse from Christopher Marlowe and Thomas Kyd whose tragedies *Tamburlaine the Great* and *The Spanish Tragedy* were the first in blank verse to appear on the public stage in 1587–8. As George T. Wright explains, 'until late in the sixteenth century, a play without rhyme would have seemed very odd to an English audience' (1988: 96).

Regular blank verse has an affected, unnatural quality, which characterizes some of the speeches in the work of Marlowe and Kyd, and some of Shakespeare's early plays. As writers became more experienced and experimental with the form, they began to introduce metrical variants, which make the verse more conversational and allow for the emphasis of particular words and phrases.

Most of Shakespeare's plays are written in a mixture of verse and prose, ranging from *Henry VI Parts 1 and 3* (*c.* 1591), *Richard II* (*c.* 1595) and *King John* (*c.*1596) which are written entirely in verse to *The Merry Wives of Windsor* (*c.*1600) which is 90 per cent prose. *As You Like It* is quite evenly balanced between prose (42.6 per cent) and verse (57.4 per cent) (Craig and Greatley-Hirsch, 2017: 71).

The conventions of prose

There are certain common conventions governing the use of prose in Shakespeare's plays. Certain characters tend to speak prose: comic characters, servants, clowns, working men and foreigners, those who are drunk or mad. Certain situations seem to demand or eschew prose. As Brian Vickers details, 'no serious or dangerous conspiracies are plotted in prose'; 'no important person in Shakespeare dies speaking prose'; 'no serious love affairs are conducted or concluded in prose' (1985: 389–90).

The use of prose as a medium for comic dialogue was partly the result of its perception as an inferior medium of expression to that of verse, more suited to the everyday themes and characters of comedy than the heightened subject matter and noble figures of tragedy and chronicle. In *The Arte of English Poesie,* George Puttenham describes verse as a superior medium to prose, both in its aesthetic qualities and in its capacity for pithy and fluid expression (1598: 5–6). He also asserts that verse is the medium best suited to subjects of import, describing it as the medium most appropriate for writing about the lives of 'Princes, and of the great monarchs of the world' (1589: 5–6).

These are the standard conventions of prose; and Shakespeare does, in general, adhere to most of the basic conventions of class distinction, madness etc. However, as his writing career progresses we find an increasing freedom in his use of the two mediums. The characteristic division between verse and prose becomes increasingly blurred as the two mediums begin to interact in a far more complex and dramatically effective manner, and as Shakespeare makes use of prose for a greater variety of expression, increasingly using it for characters from the upper classes and main plots – Hal in the *Henry IV* plays, *Henry V*, Brutus in *Julius Caesar* and some of the noble characters in *As You Like It.*

John Lyly and Euphues

John Lyly was an English dramatist and prose writer of the late sixteenth century (a contemporary of Shakespeare's). Robert Miola suggests that it was from Lyly that Shakespeare 'learned to write sophisticated, musical, rhetorical prose' (2000: 68). Between 1578 and 1580 he wrote a novel entitled *Euphues,* which was one of the most influential works of its time. The novel was written in an extremely artificial and highly rhetorical mode characterized by alliteration (the repetition of consonant sounds in close proximity), assonance (the repetition of vowel sounds in nearby words), antithesis (two opposing ideas put together in parallel clauses or sentences), and symmetry (balanced phrases). It was not only Lyly's novels, but also his major plays such as *Campaspe* (1584) and *Endymion* (1591) that featured this elevated prose style. However, as will be explored, there is a clear distinction between the noble and common characters in these plays; between rhetorical, courtly speech and colloquial or pastoral registers, something that Shakespeare also exploits in *As You Like It*.

A classical education

The rhetoric that Shakespeare found in Lyly, he would also have learned from his education. The education system at the Elizabethan grammar schools was a humanist one, based on the work of the Dutch scholar Erasmus. The curriculum was mainly Latin in focus, and students studied texts including the Roman comic dramatists Terence and Plautus, the Roman tragedian Seneca, and the poets Ovid, Virgil, Juvenal and Persius. This education would have introduced Shakespeare to countless Roman myths, most notably through Ovid's *Metamorphoses,* Virgil's *Aeneid* and the plays of Seneca.

Shakespeare's plays abound with references to these classical texts and *As You Like It* is no exception. One of the most obvious classical references comes in the form of Rosalind's choice of disguise when entering the Forest of Arden:

> ROSALIND
> I'll have no worse a name than Jove's own page;
> And therefore look you call me Ganymede.
>
> (1.3.121–2)

Ganymede was a beautiful Trojan prince with whom Zeus fell in love, abducting him in the form of an eagle, to serve as cup-bearer to the gods. References to Ganymede appear in both Ovid's *Metamorphoses* (10.152–161) and Virgil's *Aeneid* (1.28; 5.253). The choice of name, as many of the original audience would have been aware, has resonances of homoerotic desire. The word Ganymede was used in the sixteenth century to refer to young men who were the object of male homosexual passion. Although Shakespeare would have found this assumed name in his source material, it is significant that he chose to keep it. It draws attention to the potential homoeroticism inherent in the boy player, dressed as a woman on the Renaissance stage. As Mario DiGangi suggests, it also 'brings into sharp relief the discordant aspects of Rosalind's enactment of Ganymede, by means of which female homoerotic desire (Celia's for Rosalind) and male homoerotic desire (Orlando's for Ganymede) are both finally rejected' (DiGangi, 1996: 271).

The final marriage ceremony at the end of the play is graced by the figure of Hymen, whether (as discussed above) a theophany or a figure embodied by one of the other characters. Hymen was the god of marriage ceremonies and is referred to in Ovid's *Metamorphoses* (4.758–764; 9.762–797; 10.1–7). There are also brief references to countless figures from mythology throughout *As You Like It*, mostly using their Roman names. A number appear in Orlando's love poetry to Rosalind:

> Nature presently distill'd
> Helen's cheek, but not her heart,
> Cleopatra's majesty,
> Atalanta's better part,
> Sad Lucretia's modesty.
>
> (3.2.141–5)

The poem references:

- **Helen** (commonly known as Helen of Troy) (Virgil, 2.567–603): Daughter of Zeus and Leda; married to Menelaus, she was abducted by Paris, initiating the Trojan War.
- **Cleopatra** (Plutarch's *Lives of the Noble Grecians and Romans*): Cleopatra was the last active ruler of the Ptolemaic dynasty in Egypt.
- **Atalanta** (Ovid, 10.560–704): A virgin huntress, who refused to marry any man who could not beat her in a race.
- **Lucretia** (otherwise known as Lucrece) (Ovid, *Fasti*; Livy, *History of Rome*): Wife of Tarquin; raped by Sextus, after which, having told her husband, she killed herself.

Rosalind responds in 4.1, in her 'tutoring' of Orlando, with an equally erudite series of classical references, commenting satirically on ancient myths of devotion:

ROSALIND
   Troilus had his brains dashed out with a Grecian club, yet he did what he could to die before, and he is one of the patterns of

love. Leander, he would have lived many a fair year, though Hero had turned nun, if it had not been for a hot midsummer night; for, good youth, he went but forth to wash him in the Hellespont and, being taken with the cramp, was drowned, and the foolish coroners of that age found it was Hero of Sestos.

(4.1.89–97)

Here we find references to:

- **Troilus** (Homer, *Iliad* and Chaucer's *Troilus and Criseyde*): Son of King Priam of Troy; killed by Achilles. Fell in love with Cressida who was taken from Troy to the Greek camp.
- **Hero and Leander** (Ovid, *Heroides*): Hero was a priestess of Aphrodite who lived on Sestos. Leander was a young man from Abydos who fell in love with her and swam the Hellespont each night to be with her. He drowned one night in the rough waters and she threw herself from a tower when she learnt of his death.

The setting of the play is not specific. The court, with its professional fool seems Renaissance in style; Charles the Wrestler, when speaking about Duke Senior describes him as living 'like the old Robin Hood of England', implying a post-medieval setting; and yet, the characters frequently exclaim to the classical gods, such as Cupid, the god of love and desire; Jupiter or Jove, the king of the gods and Hercules, son of Jupiter, famous for his strength and courage:

- CELIA Why, cousin, why, Rosalind! Cupid have mercy! Not a word? (1.3.1–2)
- ROSALIND O Jupiter, how weary are my spirits! (2.4.1)
- ROSALIND Jove, Jove, this shepherd's passion
    Is much upon my fashion! (2.4.56–7)
- ROSALIND Now Hercules be thy speed, young man! (1.2.201)

Classical rhetoric

When studying classical texts, Shakespeare and his contemporaries were not only absorbing the myths and stories; they were also studying and emulating the use of language: style, grammar and rhetoric. Rhetoric was taught in the Elizabethan grammar school, the term meaning 'the art or study of using language effectively and persuasively'. It was taught primarily as a skill of argument for use in debate or public speaking. As Brian Vickers asserts, 'every person who had a grammar-school education in Europe between Ovid and Pope knew by heart, familiarly, up to a hundred figures, by their right names' (1971: 86).

The five key areas of rhetorical training were:

- *elocutio* – style
- *inventio* – development of an argument
- *dispositio* – the organization of an argument
- *memoria* – the use of memory
- *pronuntiatio* – the delivery of an argument

The latter two are concerned with delivery. When thinking about Shakespeare's writing we are thus interested in *elocutio*, *inventio* and *dispositio*.

Dispositio is concerned with the arrangement of writing. In classical orations this meant a system as follows:

1 *exordium* – introduction – in which one announces the subject of the discourse.
2 *narratio* – statement of facts – the speaker provides a narrative account of the issue at hand.
3 *partitio* – division – the speaker outlines what will follow.
4 *confirmatio* – proof – the speaker offers logical arguments as proof.
5 *refutatio* – refutation – the speaker answers the counterarguments.
6 *peroratio* – conclusion – the speaker sums up.

This is particularly pertinent to the writing of formal debates rather than drama; however, as Quentin Skinner has shown, there are numerous speeches within the Shakespeare canon that adhere to the classical rules of judicial debate (2014: 66).

Inventio is concerned with *what* an author would say rather than *how* this might be said – the way in which a writer constructs an argument or instigates persuasion. The ways in which a speaker might appeal to an audience were threefold: *pathos*, *logos* and *ethos*. *Pathos* is an emotional appeal, using the strategies of empathy and sympathy to sway an audience. *Logos* is a rational appeal, using evidence and factual examples. *Ethos* is an ethical appeal by which the speaker convinces the audience of the credibility of their argument. Shakespeare makes use of these different rhetorical appeals in almost all of his plays, particularly in set speeches. We see these different modes of appeal in operation in 1.3 of *As You Like It*, where Rosalind and Celia both appeal to Duke Frederick against Rosalind's banishment. Rosalind begins by using *ethos* to convince Frederick that she possesses self-knowledge and sanity and is convinced that she has never wronged him:

> If with myself I hold intelligence,
> Or have acquaintance with mine own desires,
> If that I do not dream, or be not frantic –
> As I do trust I am not – then, dear uncle,
> Never so much as in a thought unborn
> Did I offend your highness.
>
> (1.3.44–9)

Following his assertion 'Thou art thy father's daughter, there's enough', she uses *logos* to refute his claim with facts:

> So was I when your highness took his dukedom;
> So was I when your highness banished him.
> Treason is not inherited, my lord,
>
> (1.3.56–8)

Celia, by contrast, seems more emotional in her appeal to her father, beginning by blaming him, declaring herself a traitor and then describing her close relationship with Rosalind:

> We still have slept together,
> Rose at an instant, learned, played, ate together,
> And whereso'er we went, like Juno's swans,
> Still we went coupled and inseparable.
>
> (1.3.70–4)

Elocutio concerns the *way* in which ideas are expressed and is concerned with rhetoric. Some rhetorical devices are quite familiar to those who study literature today: assonance (repetition of vowel sounds), alliteration (repetition of consonants), onomatopoeia (words that sound like the thing they describe), metaphor (referring to one thing as another); simile (comparing one thing with another); personification (referring to inanimate objects or abstractions as though they were human); oxymoron (placing two ordinarily opposing terms adjacent to one another); antithesis (juxtaposition of contrasting ideas). Others are more unusual and unfamiliar; however, once we recognize them, we can find them in abundance in Shakespeare's plays; and once we find them, we start to see patterns relating to character and situation.

Two common devices used by Shakespeare are 'metonymy' and 'synecdoche'. These are easily confused, but, as we will see, are distinctive. Synecdoche is the practice of using a part of something to refer to the whole – 'my wheels' to mean 'my car' for example. Metonymy is the use of one thing to represent another that is closely connected to it, a common example being 'the press' to refer to journalists (the press being the machine used for printing newspapers). Examples from *As You Like It* include:

- 'Within this roof / The enemy of all your graces lives' (2.3.17–18) (roof being used as a synecdoche for house)
- 'as doublet and hose ought to show itself courageous to petticoat' (2.4.6–7) (items of clothing associated with men and women being used as a metonym for their gender)

The other most common rhetorical devices in Shakespeare are those of repetition. These are particularly common in the early plays (in particular the early history plays) and in public orations. These highly patterned forms are particularly noticeable in verse speeches, where the repetitions often come at the beginning or endings of verse lines as well as phrases, but they can also be found in Shakespeare's more rhetorical prose. Some of the most common which are found *in As You Like It are* listed in Table 1.

TABLE 1. Key Rhetorical Figures

anaphora	Repetition of the same word or groups of words at the beginning of successive clauses	So was I when your highness took his dukedom; So was I when your highness banished him. (1.3.56–7)
epistrophe	Repetition of the same word or words at the ends of successive clauses	I'll have no father, if you be not he. I'll have no husband, if you be not he. (5.4.120–1)
anadiplosis	Repetition of the last word of one clause at the start of the next	For your brother and my sister no sooner met but they looked; no sooner looked but they loved; no sooner loved but they sighed; no sooner sighed but they asked one another the reason, no sooner knew the reason but they sought the remedy. (5.2.31–5)
epanalepsis	Repetition at the end of a clause of the word that occurred at the beginning	Of what kind should this cock come of? (2.7.91)
antimetabole	Repetition that turns the sentence around	'Tis true, for those that she makes fair she scarce makes honest, and those that she makes honest she makes very ill-favouredly. (1.2.37–9)
ploce	Repetition of a single word for emphasis	Foul is most foul, being foul to be a scoffer (3.5.63)

chiasmus	A pair of words or ideas arranged in successive clauses in inverse order	Your gentleness shall force More than your force move us to gentleness. (2.7.103–4)
isocolon	Repetition of phrases or clauses of equal length	DUKE SENIOR If there be truth in sight, you are my daughter. ORLANDO If there be truth in sight, you are my Rosalind. (5.4.116–17)

Shakespeare's biblical language

As part of his grammar-school education, Shakespeare would also have become readily familiar with what Steven Marx refers to as 'the most powerful cultural influence of its time' – the Bible (Marx, 2000: 3). In addition to studying passages from the scriptures, Shakespeare would also have attended church on a weekly basis, during which he would have heard passages from the scriptures read aloud. Evidence of Shakespeare's familiarity with the Bible, and with the Anglican Book of Common Prayer, is present throughout his work, in the form of biblical quotations, quotations from Psalms and references to biblical stories.

Whilst many of Shakespeare's biblical references are allusions rather than direct quotations, in other cases, the wording seems to point directly to Shakespeare's use of the Geneva Bible, first published in 1560. We find allusions to the Garden of Eden (Genesis) – in the concept of the forest as a place where the foresters 'feel . . . not the penalty of Adam', the extremes of climate change to which Eden became subject after the Fall of Man – and to the parable of the Prodigal son (Luke 15) in Orlando's lines – 'Shall I keep your hogs and eat husks with them? What prodigal portion have I spent that I should come to such penury?' In the parable, the younger son wastes his inheritance with 'riotous living' and, reduced to poverty, finds a job as a swineherd and is so hungry that he 'would fain have filled his belly with the husks that the swine did eat' (Luke 15.16,

Geneva Bible). Orlando asserts that he has not wasted his inheritance and should not be reduced to such a condition. Jaques twice makes explicit references to stories of the Old Testament – the plague on the firstborn sons of Egypt in Exodus: 'I'll rail against the first-born of Egypt' (2.5.53–4) and the tale of Noah's Ark in Genesis: 'There is sure another flood toward, and these couples are coming to the ark' (5.4.35–6). Celia refers to Judas's betrayal of Christ in the Garden of Gethsemane: 'Marry, his kisses are Judas's own children' (3.4.7–8) as told in the gospels of Matthew, Mark and Luke.

Verbal parallels to passages in the Geneva Bible can also be identified throughout the play, as shown in Table 2. One of the most extensive passages of biblical symbolism comes, as Lieke Stelling identifies, in the narrative of the conversion of Oliver, in his account in 4.3, where his 'wickedness is represented by a serpent and a lioness preying on his sleeping body', these being the two animals depicted as evil in Psalm 91.13: 'Thou shalt walk upon the lion and asp' (Geneva Bible). Stelling also identifies in Oliver's language, 'the language of Christian conversion and salvation': 'since my conversion / So sweetly tastes, being the thing I am' (4.3.135–6) (Stelling, 2019: 68–9).

The aim of this introduction is to provide the context: print, theatrical and literary for Shakespeare's composition of *As You Like It*. The following chapters will explore the language of the play itself in more detail.

TABLE 2. Echoes from the Geneva Bible

ROSALIND Why wither shall we go? (1.3.103)	'for whither thou goest, I will go' (Ruth 1.16)
ADAM He that doth the ravens feed / Yea, providently caters for the sparrow (2.3.43–4)	'Consider the ravens: for they neither sow nor reap . . . and yet God feedeth them' (Luke 12.24) 'Are not two sparrows sold for a farthing, and one of them shall not fall on the ground without your Father' (Matthew 10.29)
ROSALIND I must comfort the weaker vessel (2.4.6)	'giving honour unto the woman, as unto the weaker vessel' (1 Peter 3.7)
TOUCHSTONE Truly, the tree yields bad fruit (3.2.113)	'a corrupt tree bringeth forth evil fruit' (Matthew 7.17)
ROSALIND No. I will not cast away my physic but on those that are sick. (3.2.345–6)	'The whole need not a physician, but they that are sick' (Matthew 9.12)
PHOEBE Thou hast my love, is not that neighbourly? (3.5.91)	'Thou shalt love thy neighbour as thyself' (Matthew 19.19)
SILVIUS That I shall think it a most plenteous crop / To glean the broken ears after the man / That the main harvest reaps' (3.5.102–4)	'gather ears of corn after him, in whose sight I find favour' (Ruth 2.2)

CHAPTER ONE

Language in Context

This chapter examines the writing and language of *As You Like It* in the context of notions of classical comedy, festive comedy and pastoralism. It explores Shakespeare's sources for the play and the question of the play's setting. It then considers the characters of the play and some of the actors for whom Shakespeare wrote *As You Like It* – the impact of the boy actor on the interpretation of Rosalind and Celia; the figure of the clown or fool and the actors who might have played the role of Touchstone and the literary figure of the malcontent and its influence on the character of Jaques. Finally, it considers the theatrical devices of metatheatre and masque, and the language used to express these devices within the play.

Genre

The title of the First Folio of Shakespeare's work – *Mr William Shakespeares Tragedies, Comedies and Histories* – created a tripartite genre division that has shaped the way in which people think about Shakespeare plays. *As You Like It* is listed as a comedy. The genre of comedy, like that of tragedy, is one that Shakespeare and his fellow dramatists inherited from classical literature. As discussed in the introduction, Shakespeare's humanist education would have introduced him predominantly to Roman models for these forms, notably Plautus and Terence for the genre of comedy, alongside Seneca for tragedy.

What is a comedy?

The genre of comedy emerged in Ancient Greece in around 486 BCE. The most famous proponent of early Greek comedy was Aristophanes, whose plays include *The Wasps, The Birds, The Frogs, The Clouds* – the titles of which provide an indication of the characterization of the Chorus (usually a group of twenty-four men, embodying these abstractions). Early Greek comedy was extremely bawdy and characters wore costumes that made them appear fat, and naked from the waist down. These comedies were mainly political satires, mocking the powerful institutions of the time. The language was full of sexual innuendo and scatological puns. However, as Greek comedy developed it became less satirical and more romantic, focusing more on domestic themes – family relationships, lost children found, sexual encounters, love, and marriage – all of which may sound familiar to those accustomed to reading Shakespearean comedies.

The Romans were heavily influenced by Greek New Comedy and the Elizabethans, in turn, took inspiration from the leading Roman comic dramatists.

Shakespeare would have studied the plays of Plautus and Terence at school, and would have been expected to analyse their work in detail, as this passage on teaching the work of Terence, from Desiderius Erasmus's *De Ratione Studii*, suggests:

> Before translating this he should first of all discuss briefly the author's circumstances, his talent, and the elegance of his language. Then he should mention how much enjoyment and instruction may be had from reading comedy and its laws ... He should be careful to point out the type of metre ... he should carefully draw their attention to any purple passage, archaism, neologism, Graecism, any obscure or verbose expression, and abrupt or confused order, any etymology, figure of speech, or rhetorical passages, or embellishment or corruption
>
> (trans. Thompson, 1978: 682–3)

One can see from this passage that as well as providing a model for the use of metre (poetic rhythm), language and rhetoric, reading comedy was intended to provide both 'enjoyment' and 'instruction'. This is echoed by Philip Sidney in his *Defense of Poesie*, a key piece of Renaissance literary criticism, written in around 1580, though not published until 1595. Sidney, defending poetry and drama against Puritan accusations about their negative influence, argues that comedy has the potential to provide moral education, by serving as a negative exemplum:

> the Comedy is an imitation of the common errors of our life, which he representeth in the most ridiculous and scornful sort that may be: so as it is impossible that any beholder can be content to be such a one.
>
> (1595: E4v–E4r)

It is interesting to consider *As You Like It,* and indeed Shakespeare's other comedies, in the light of this statement. Characters do make mistakes, some of which are laughable, but in many cases the protagonists of Shakespeare's comedies are highly attractive figures, articulate and witty. Indeed, we might see Shakespeare's tragic protagonists as embodying negative qualities far more than his comic ones.

The Elizabethans' conception of comedy as a genre also came partly from Greek and Roman literary theory, most notably the *Poetics* of Aristotle, written in the third century BCE, and often considered the earliest piece of literary criticism, and the essays attributed to Aeilius Donatus – 'On Comedy' and 'On Drama' – the latter of which is now understood to be by another Latin writer, Euanthius. Euanthius' description of comedy sits in opposition to Sidney's, and is, perhaps, more fitting in suggesting the potential instructive function of Shakespeare's two genres – 'And in tragedy the kind of life is shown that is to be shunned; while in comedy the kind is shown that is to be sought after' (trans. O. B. Hardison Jr., 1974: 45). Certainly, the behaviour of characters like Rosalind, Celia and Orlando, and even Touchstone and Jaques seems far more palatable than that of figures like Iago and even Othello.

If we look at some further classical definitions of comedy, we can begin to see how Shakespeare's drama adheres to or breaks away from classical expectations. According to Aristotle, comedy is

> where those who, in the piece, are the deadliest enemies . . . quit the stage as friends at the close, and no one slays or is slain.
>
> (Harmon, 2005: 45)

Euanthius similarly tells us that comedy ends with:

> the resolution of the course of events so that there is a happy ending which is made evident to all by the recognition of past events

He expands:

> in comedy . . . the dangers are slight, and the ends of the action are happy . . . the beginning is troubled, the end tranquil
> (trans. O. B. Hardison Jr., 1974: 305).

If we think about these definitions in relation to *As You Like It*, the first seems broadly true. The play begins with two pairs of brothers as 'deadliest enemies': Oliver and Orlando and Duke Senior and Duke Frederick. Certainly by the end of the play Oliver and Orlando are fully reconciled, and although we do not see a reconciliation between the dukes, Jaques de Boys delivers news that Duke Frederick has been 'converted', 'bequeathing' the crown to his brother and restoring the lands of those exiled with him (5.4.159–61). In terms of people being 'slain', we do not see any deaths, although we do hear, albeit in a rather casual comment, that Charles the Wrestler has broken the ribs of three young men so that 'there is little hope of life' in them (1.2.121–2). In consideration of the second definition, we can reasonably say that there is a resolution, leading to a happy ending for most characters. Regarding the third definition, there is, perhaps, more of a question mark. The 'ends of the action' are broadly happy, but we might question whether the 'dangers are slight'. Indeed, as in many of Shakespeare's comedies, some of the dangers encountered by the characters bring them into close proximity with death. Orlando's brother tries to kill him on two occasions, firstly by paying Charles the Wrestler to fight with him, and secondly by planning to burn his lodgings (2.3.23). Rosalind is threatened with death by her uncle, if she comes within twenty miles of the court (1.3.40–2). The trip to Arden is clearly dangerous for the two young women and proves nearly fatal for Adam. Indeed, some productions of the play have had Adam die shortly after Orlando brings him to the duke (making sense of the fact that he does not appear again after this point in the play). In many senses the first half of the play might almost seem like a tragedy. It's not really until Act 3, with the arrival of spring, that we begin to see the traits of a comedy emerging – in disguise, confusion, mistaken identity and love.

This is one way in which Shakespeare departs from classical tradition. One is never going to mistake a Greek or Roman comedy for a Greek or Roman tragedy at any point. However, often Shakespeare's comedies include characters under threat and sometimes close to death. Indeed, even in his early comedies – *The Two Gentlemen of Verona* (1589) and *The Comedy of Errors* (1590) – Shakespeare was already combining serious matter with comedy, as were many of his contemporaries. Only a year or so after the composition of *As You Like It,* one of Shakespeare's characters – Polonius in *Hamlet* – comments satirically on the multiplicity of genres on the stage when he speaks of the players, newly arrived in Elsinore, as 'The best actors in the world, either for tragedy, comedy, history, pastoral, pastoral-comical, historical-pastoral, scene individable or poem unlimited' (*Ham* 2.2.333–6). As early as the 1580s, Philip Sidney was complaining about plays that:

> be neither right tragedies, nor right comedies, mingling kings and clowns, not because the matter so carrieth it, but thrust in clowns by head and shoulders, to play a part in majestical matters, with neither decency nor discretion, so as neither the admiration and commiseration, nor the right sportfulness, is by their mongrel tragicomedy obtained.
>
> (Sidney, 1585: I1v–I1r)

The other major influence on Shakespeare's conception of the genre of comedy would have been the vernacular drama of the later 1500s. Plays such as *Ralph Roister Doister* (*c.*1552) and *Gammer Gurton's Needle* (*c.*1567), which were written for the Universities and Inns of Courts, might well have been read, seen or even performed by the Shakespeare as a boy. These comedies, as Lawrence Danson points out, were themselves 'derived from the Roman plays of Plautus and Terence', blending the classical tradition with 'English humour and plots' (2000: 49). They were farcical and vulgar, with coarse physical humour, much like their Latin counterparts. More sophisticated were the comedies of John Lyly. As we have already seen, Lyly's prose style was influential on Shakespeare's use of language. As Danson suggests, there are a number of other ways in which Lyly's writing influenced Shakespeare – in the interwoven strands of narrative, the range of characters, the Ovidian themes and comedy based on 'same-sex wooing' (2000: 50–1). Lyly's plays were essentially romantic comedies in which confusion and chaos in the affairs of love are finally resolved into a 'happy' ending, often with multiple marriages.

It's not clear whether an Elizabethan audience would have known in advance the genre of a play that they were going to see. The most common avenue for getting information about what plays were to be performed in London on a particular date were playbills, which would have been posted around the city. However, given the fact that no playbills from the period survive, it is difficult to ascertain the type of information that these bills would have conveyed. Tiffany Stern, drawing on a range of sources to reconstruct the nature of playbills asserts that whilst the title of a play was 'a given', 'the naming of the genre of play to be performed went in and out of fashion' (2009: 56–7). Of course, the name of the play itself might have given away its genre. In keeping with other of Shakespeare's comedies – *Much Ado About Nothing, Twelfth Night or What You Will, All's Well that Ends Well* – *As You Like It* has a title that suggests a certain flippancy. However, we cannot be certain that the titles of the plays that have come down to us are those under which they were originally performed.

There is some evidence that theatres might have draped the stage with black cloth for the performance of a tragedy, although Andrew Gurr finds the thought 'frankly alarming' asking: 'Would a set of more decorative hangings lead the audience to expect a comedy? If a tragedy was signaled by the stage's being hung with black, how might a tragicomedy have been signaled? Why was it thought necessary to remove the element of suspense from a play's conclusion?' (2011: 71–2). These are all pertinent questions that call into doubt the regular use of such a practice. Nevertheless, Shakespeare's Globe theatre played with the possibility of this convention for Thea Sharrock's production of *As You Like It* in 2009. When the audience entered the theatre the stage was draped with black, implying, to those familiar with the convention, a tragic theme, only for these sheets to be ripped down on the characters' entry to Arden. This exploitation of possible Early Modern playhouse practice served to emphasize the play's movement from a darker, more tragic tone to one of playfulness and celebration.

Festive comedy

We will look now at a very particular definition of comedy associated with *As You Like It,* that of festive comedy. Modern criticism has tended to divide Shakespeare's comedies into groups including the early apprentice comedies – *The Comedy of Errors, Two Gentlemen of Verona, Love's Labour's Lost, The Taming of the Shrew;* the later problem comedies, including *All's Well That Ends Well* and *Measure for Measure;* and the final Romances – *Pericles, Cymbeline, The Winter's Tale and The Tempest.* The heyday of Shakespeare's comedy is seen as the middle period, from *Midsummer Night's Dream* to *Twelfth Night* – encompassing *Much Ado About Nothing, The Merchant of Venice* and *As You Like It.* These plays have often been defined as 'festive' comedies, most famously by C. L. Barber in his seminal book *Shakespeare's Festive Comedy (1959).*

In the Early Modern period, the calendar was firmly tied to the church, with saints' days and feasts playing a major role. Some festivals were linked to Christian tradition, others derived from earlier pagan holidays. These included St Valentine's Day, Shrove Tuesday, May Day, Hallowmas, Christmas, Twelfth Night and Epiphany. Such festive occasions were readily associated with excess of food, drink and sex, and often involved masquing and disguise. The festivals permitted a release from certain social conventions and rules. Barber tells us that: 'Holiday, for the Elizabethan sensibility implied a contrast with "everyday" . . . the release of that one day was understood to be a temporary licence, a misrule which implied rule' (Barber, 1959: 10). This is an important factor: the knowledge that, after the disruption a return to order will occur.

In his book, Barber undertook a major study of Shakespeare's plays in which he emphasized the elements of revelry and holiday. He asserts that, 'the social form of Elizabethan holidays contributed to the dramatic form of festive comedy' (1959: 4). In *As You Like It,* as in other of Shakespeare's middle comedies, we are transported, along with some of the characters, to a world apart from their normal existence. In *As You Like It* most of the characters end up in the Forest of Arden, a temporary place of sanctuary and, in some senses, holiday. In 4.1 Rosalind declares herself to be in a holiday mood:

ROSALIND
Come, woo me, woo me, for now I am in a holiday humour and like enough to consent.

(4.1.62–3)

Significantly, in *As You Like It,* the forest is also a place where the social hierarchies of the court are turned upside down, much as they were during festivities. During the twelve days of Christmas, for example, the traditional social hierarchy in a court, noble household or Inn of Court was subverted, with a lower member appointed the Lord of Misrule and given licence to organize boisterous activities and to make fun of his social superiors. In *As You Like It* traditional roles are reversed when Rosalind, disguised as a man, is able to tutor Orlando in the realities of love; when Celia, the duke's daughter temporarily takes on the role of a shepherdess; and when Duke Senior, banished from the court, is revealed to be living like 'the old Robin Hood of England' in the woods. However, significantly, by the end of the play, disorder has led to order – a return to the social norms of heterosexual marriage in which the woman gives herself to her husband ('To you I give myself, for I am yours'; 5.4.115); an end to conflict and usurpation, and a restoration of the rightful order, with Duke Senior once more on the throne; and a return from Arden to the court.

Like many of Shakespeare's comedies, *As You Like It* revolves around the contrast between the everyday world, as represented by the court, and a festive location emblematic of escape and transformation, as embodied in the Forest of Arden; a contrast between the artificial and the natural world, between a place where violence prevails and one where the banished Duke and his followers live in harmony, and between a corrupt dictatorship: an 'envious' place of 'peril' and 'painted pomp' (2.1.3–4) and a place where hierarchies have been dissolved, the banished Duke referring to his men as 'co-mates and brothers in exile' (2.1.1).

Pastoral

Another genre which is of significance in relation to *As You Like It* is that of the pastoral, predominantly a poetic genre. The pastoral genre originated in Ancient Greece and Rome, in the works of

Hesiod, Theocritus and Virgil. The genre presents a fictionalized, idealized conception of rural life, with shepherds and shepherdesses living a simple but harmonious existence away from the corruptions of the court. The genre became popular in the Renaissance, with English pastorals being modelled on those of Italy and Spain, which, in turn, looked back to classical literature. The first English pastoral was Edmund Spenser's *The Shepheardes Calendar* (1579). In addition to the work of Spenser, we find Robert Greene's prose works *Pandosto* (1588) and *Menaphon* or *Greene's Arcadia* (1589), Philip Sidney's *Arcadia* (1590) and Thomas Lodge's *Rosalynde* (1590), the direct source for *As You Like It*. Defining the pastoral genre has proved difficult, but we can identify certain features of both classical and Renaissance pastoral literature – the two worlds, rural and urban, set in opposition; idealized simplicity set against complexity; the evocation of a Golden Age; shepherds who live a life of ease; Petrarchan shepherd lovers (a young shepherd lamenting his unrequited love for a frequently scornful shepherdess as was characteristic of the poetry of the Italian poet Petrarch); old shepherds commenting upon the foolish love of the young; cross-gendered disguise, and travel.

Many of these elements are features of *As You Like It*. The Forest of Arden is set directly against the world of the court, both by Duke Senior – 'Are not these woods / More free from peril than the envious court' (2.1.3–4) – and by Touchstone and Corin in their 3.2 conversation (11–82), with the forest depicted as simpler and less sophisticated, but also less threatening than the court (although, as many commentators have pointed out, there remain elements of hierarchy and threat in the forest). The Golden Age is referenced directly by Charles the Wrestler, who tells Oliver that Duke Senior and those who have joined him in the forest 'fleet the time carelessly as they did in the golden world' (1.1.112–13). Two of the characters most strongly influenced by this genre are Phoebe and Silvius. In some respects they can be seen as stock figures in this tradition – the love-struck shepherd, idealizing his cruel, scornful mistress.

In the first scene in which we see Silvius, he is in conversation with the older shepherd Corin:

CORIN
That is the way to make her scorn you still.

SILVIUS
O Corin, that thou knewst how I do love her!
CORIN
I partly guess; for I have loved ere now.
SILVIUS
No, Corin, being old, thou canst not guess,
Though in thy youth thou wast as true a lover
As ever sighed upon a midnight pillow.
But if thy love were ever like to mine –
As sure I think did never man love so –
How many actions most ridiculous
Hast thou been drawn to by thy fantasy?
CORIN
Into a thousand that I have forgotten.
SILVIUS
O, thou didst then never love so heartily!
If thou rememb'rest not the slightest folly
That ever love did make thee run into,
Thou hast not loved.
Or if thou hast not sat as I do now,
Wearying thy hearer in thy mistress' praise,
Thou hast not loved.
Or if thou hast not broke from company
Abruptly as my passion now makes me,
Thou hast not loved.
O Phoebe, Phoebe, Phoebe!

(2.4.19–40)

He seems like a pastoral stereotype with his exaggerated expression of his unrequited love. Silvius also speaks in highly patterned, poetic language. As discussed in the introduction, verse is often the preserve of characters from the upper echelons of society, and therefore it might seem unusual for a character like a shepherd to speak in rhetorical verse. However, this is part of Silvius' status as a stock pastoral romantic figure – a Petrarchan lover. Indeed, Corin seems to comment on the artificiality of Phoebe and Silvius' relationship, when he says to Rosalind in 3.4:

CORIN
If you will see a pageant truly played,

Between the pale complexion of true love
And the red glow of scorn and proud disdain,
Go hence a little and I shall conduct you,
If you will mark it.

(48–52)

Later, in 5.2 we find an even more patterned and artificial expression of love, once again led by Silvius. The verse with its repeated phrases is so patterned that it is almost song-like. Indeed Trevor Nunn set the lines to music in his 1977 RSC production.

PHOEBE
Good shepherd, tell this youth what 'tis to love.
SILVIUS
It is to be all made of sighs and tears,
And so am I for Phoebe.
PHOEBE
And I for Ganymede.
ORLANDO
And I for Rosalind.
ROSALIND
And I for no woman.
SILVIUS
It is to be all made of faith and service,
And so am I for Phoebe.
PHOEBE
And I for Ganymede.
ORLANDO
And I for Rosalind.
ROSALIND
And I for no woman.
SILVIUS
It is to be all made of fantasy,
All made of passion, and all made of wishes,
All adoration, duty and observance,
All humbleness, all patience and impatience,
All purity, all trial, all obedience,
And so am I for Phoebe.
PHOEBE
And so am I for Ganymede.

ORLANDO
And so am I for Rosalind.
ROSALIND
And so am I for no woman.
PHOEBE
If this be so, why blame you me to love you?
SILVIUS
If this be so, why blame you me to love you?
ORLANDO
If this be so, why blame you me to love you?

(5.2.79–101)

Shakespeare seems to be both indulging in and exposing the artificiality of the pastoral genre, with Rosalind herself suddenly breaking the refrain to question 'Who do you speak to, "Why blame you me to love you?"' and finally declaring the episode to be like 'the howling of Irish wolves' (5.2.105–6).

It is, of course, part of the pastoral romance tradition that all of the lovers end up paired by the end of the play; Rosalind with Orlando, Celia with Oliver, Touchstone with Audrey, and, in spite of her apparent resistance throughout, Phoebe with Silvius. This can seem uncomfortable to a modern audience, but Shakespeare's audiences may have been more accustomed to, and accepting of, the literary convention.

Source and setting

Shakespeare and Thomas Lodge

As discussed, Lodge's *Rosalynde* is the major source for the much of the plot, and many of the characters, of *As You Like It* and is firmly in the pastoral tradition. Shakespeare took many of the stories for his plays from pre-existing sources. What is interesting is the ways in which he transformed that material from one genre to another (here from narrative fiction to drama), the changes, excisions and additions that he made in doing so and the verbal echoes that remain.

From his source material, Shakespeare took the basic story of *As You Like It,* albeit changing the names of most of the major characters: King Torismond becomes Duke Frederick; King Gerismond, Duke Senior; Alinda, Torismond's daughter, Celia; Rosader, the youngest son of Sir John of Bordeaux, Orlando; Bordeaux's oldest son Saladyne, Oliver; Montanus becomes Silvius and Corydon, Corin. Only Rosalind and Phoebe keep the same names. Lodge's story begins, as does Shakespeare's play, with one leader having usurped the other, who is now in exile in the Forest of Arden; two brothers in conflict; a wrestling match, won by the younger brother; and the two daughters being banished and disguising themselves as Ganymede and Aliena. Thereafter we find parallels in the wooing of the disdainful shepherdess Phoebe by her lover, overseen by Ganymede and Aliena; Phoebe falling in love with Rosalynde as Ganymede; the younger brother's rescue of the elder from a lion; the marriage of the elder brother to the usurping leader's daughter and the final restoration of the exiled leader.

In some ways, the proximity of Shakespeare's play to his source material focuses us more astutely on the differences. In terms of character relationships, Shakespeare makes the two leaders brothers, adding a family dimension to the conflict and creating a thematic parallel with the warring brothers Oliver and Orlando. In turn, this makes the characters Rosalind and Celia cousins, which reinforces the closeness of their relationship. To the characters that he found in Lodge, Shakespeare adds those of Touchstone, Jaques, Amiens, William and Audrey, Martext and Le Beau. Most of these characters contribute in some way to the comic tone of the play, most notably Touchstone and Jaques with their different brands of wit. Le Beau, William, Audrey and Martext all appear in interactions with Touchstone, all become objects of ridicule to a greater or lesser extent, and all are larger-than-life characters. These characters thus help to transform a rather dry, moralistic narrative into an entertaining, quick-witted stage comedy.

In transferring the tale from narrative prose to drama, the story gains a greater immediacy. Lengthy backstories do not work on stage, and repetition is often theatrically tedious. Shakespeare speeds up and streamlines the action, focusing on events in the Forest of Arden. He cuts out the many years at the start of the story during which Rosader and Saladyne have a protracted quarrel, with bouts of disagreement and apparent reconciliation. Once we are in the forest, the story back at court is dropped after 3.1. This obviates the need to move back and forth between different locations, concentrating the action in a single place. We do not have the imprisonment and then banishment of the Saladyne/Oliver figure, followed by his repentance and desire to seek his brother. One effect of this is that Oliver's motivation to enter the forest appears to be Duke Frederick's order to 'Bring him dead or living / Within this twelvemonth' (3.1.6–7), meaning that his repentance happens only once he is in the forest, much like the conversion of Duke Frederick, reinforcing the idea of the forest as a place of reconciliation and transformation. In addition to streamlining the time-scale and action, Shakespeare streamlines the plot-lines, placing the focus firmly on the central love plot of Rosalind and Orlando, and reducing the space given to the relationships of Phoebe and Silvius and Celia and Oliver, the latter of which forms very suddenly towards the end of the play.

In terms of tone, Shakespeare significantly lightens the mood of the story, reducing the levels of violence. In the wrestling match Charles is winded, and humiliated, but not killed. There is no attempted kidnap of Celia, as there is of Alinda. This means that unlike in Lodge's tale, where the relationship between Alinda and Saladyne is initiated by him saving her from the outlaws, Celia and Oliver experience love at first sight, the suddenness of which may seem implausible, but is suitably characteristic of a comedy. Also somewhat implausible, but characteristic of the genre, is the sudden conversion of Duke Frederick who, as Jaques de Boys relates, on arriving in the forest met 'with an old religious man' after which he 'was converted / Both from his enterprise and from the world, / His crown bequeathing to his banished brother'; 5.4.159–61). This is unlike the Lodge narrative in which Torismond is 'slaine in battaile' (Lodge, 1590: S1r).

We have already touched on some of the consequences of the conversion of a story from one genre to another (narrative prose to drama). An obvious effect is on the language itself; however, with *As You Like It,* this goes beyond a simple matter of the alteration of prose narrative into dramatic dialogue. Lodge's register and style is quite different from Shakespeare's. *Rosalynde* is an episodic prose narrative, which is broken up with passages of verse and song. Although Shakespeare's play is also written in a mixture of prose, verse and song, the mediums are far more integrated. The songs in *As You Like It* are quite different in style and tone from those found in Lodge's novel. Whilst the songs in *Rosalynde* are mostly on the theme of unrequited love, attributed to individual characters as an artificial means of expressing their feelings, those in *As You Like It* are essentially folk songs (some of which may have been pre-existing popular songs), sung as a form of entertainment for other characters, much as they might be in a real rural community. The poetry in Lodge is a mixture of poetic eclogues, sonnets and love poems, all written in a serious tone. In *As You Like It,* the few poems that we do encounter are held up for ridicule – Orlando's poems with their forced rhymes and clunky rhythms (3.2.85–92, 122–51) mocked by Touchstone, and Phoebe's poetic letter to Ganymede (4.3.40–63) deliberately misinterpreted by Rosalind. Meanwhile, as we will see, verse and prose are, as in most of Shakespeare's drama, skilfully moulded together in the dramatic dialogue, with shifts in register indicative of shifts in character, mood and situation.

Lodge's novel is written in elaborate, euphuistic language, in the mode of Lyly's work discussed in the introduction. It is sententious in tone, framed by the poetic 'Schedule' left by Sir John of Bordeaux for his sons, which is strongly resonant of the advice given to Laertes by Polonius in Shakespeare's *Hamlet*:

> In choice of thrift let honour be thy gain,
> Win it by virtue and by manly might;
> In doing good estcem thy toil no pain,
> Protect the fatherless and widow's right:
> Fight for thy faith, thy Country, and thy King,
> For why? this thrift will prove a blessed thing.
>
> (Lodge, 1590: B3v, spelling modernized)

and by the final 'epilogue', presenting its moral:

> Here Gentlemen may you see in Euphues golden Legacy, that such as neglect their father's precepts, incur much prejudice; that division in Nature as it is a blemish in nurture, so 'tis a breach of good fortunes; that virtue is not measured by birth but by action; that younger brethren though inferior in years, yet may be superior to honours; that concord is the sweetest conclusion, and amity betwixt brothers more forceable than fortune.
>
> (Lodge, 1590: S2r, spelling modernized)

As You Like It, by contrast, makes little attempt at moral seriousness, the two 'commentators' within the play being Jaques and Touchstone, both of whom take a comic, satirical stance on the behaviour of their fellow human beings.

The Forest of Arden/Ardenne

Much debate has surrounded the location of the forest in *As You Like It*, notably whether it is located in England or in France; in the Forest of Arden in Warwickshire, near where Shakespeare lived, or in La Forêt d'Ardenne – a location on the border between modern France and Belgium. The latter location derives from Lodge's novel, which is set firmly in France, beginning, 'There dwelled adjoining to the city of Bordeaux a Knight of most honourable parentage' (1590: B1r). Shakespeare seems, at first glance, to have followed his source in this respect. Many of the characters at court have French names – Monsieur Le Beau, Dennis, Rowland de Boys, Jaques de Boys and Amiens; Oliver says of Orlando, 'it is the stubbornest young fellow of France' (1.1.133–4) and a number of the characters are referred to as 'Monsieur'. Although the name of the forest is spelt 'Arden' in the Folio edition, the editors of the Oxford Shakespeare (1986) chose to use the spelling 'Ardenne', on the basis that they saw 'no grounds for the argument that Shakespeare transfers the action to England, and, numerous reasons to believe that he intends us, in the opening scenes, to suppose that the action takes place out of England and, specifically, in France' (Wells, 1984: 28). For Stanley Wells, 'in these circumstances' it seemed 'perverse to choose a form of the word which is specifically English when a well-known Continental form is available' (1984: 29). However, Dusinberre argues that another name in the text, Sir Oliver Martext, 'would have located Arden, at least for the Elizabethan civil and ecclesiastical authorities, firmly in Shakespeare's Warwickshire', the name 'invok[ing] the Puritan secretaries [writers of anonymous tracts] who attacked Bishops' (2006: 58) as part of the Marprelate controversy, a war of pamphlets between a Puritan writer, who composed under the pseudonym Martin Marprelate and the Anglican church, in the late 1580s. One might also observe that when it comes to the inhabitants of the forest, characters – including Audrey, William and Corin – seem like typical English country folk.

What becomes clear, when we look at the text, is that this forest is neither that of Warwickshire nor of the Ardennes. It is a conflation of these two locations, a fantastical location, where palm trees and olive groves coexist with oak trees; lionesses and snakes with sheep and goats:

> ROSALIND
> I was seven of the nine days out of the wonder
> before you came; for look here what I found on a
> palm-tree.
>
> (3.2.170–2)

> OLIVER
> Good morrow, fair ones: pray you, if you know,
> Where in the purlieus of this forest stands
> A sheep-cote fenced about with olive trees?
>
> (4.3.74–6)

> DUKE SENIOR
> Today my Lord of Amiens and myself
> Did steal behind him as he lay along
> Under an oak, whose antique root peeps out
>
> (2.1.29–31)

> TOUCHSTONE
> Come apace, good Audrey – I will fetch
> up your goats, Audrey.
>
> (3.3.1–2)

> OLIVER
>   about his neck
> A green and gilded snake had wreathed itself,
> Who, with her head, nimble in threats, approached
> The opening of his mouth. But suddenly
> Seeing Orlando, it unlinked itself
> And with indented glides did slip away
> Into a bush; under which bush's shade
> A lioness, with udders all drawn dry,
> Lay couching, head on ground, with catlike watch,
>
> (4.3.106–14)

These incompatible descriptions are one of the factors that make the forest difficult to depict on stage, and even more so on film. In the Elizabethan playhouses, the minimal use of scenery (as discussed in the introduction) would have meant that the forest would have existed primarily in the audience's imagination, conjured by the language of the play. Without recourse to elaborate scenery it is, perhaps, easier to accept and assimilate the apparently incongruous features of the forest without having to imagine them literally co-existing. As soon as a director or designer tries to depict the forest in any kind of literal fashion they are likely to fall into difficulty. Many have thus looked for a more figurative rendering of Arden, based less on its physical features, and more on its symbolic qualities. However, whilst a minimal or figurative representation of the forest may work in the theatre, it is not easily compatible with the genre of film, which must set the action somewhere. Christine Edzard's 1992 film locates both the court and the forest in London – the latter being a riverside wasteland in London's docklands, whilst Kenneth Branagh's 2006 film is set in nineteenth-century Japan with the forest a sort of Japanese garden. The latter two films, in keepings with some contemporary productions, cut the reference to Orlando as the 'stubbornest fellow of France', which seems incompatible with an explicitly non-French setting.

If we return again to the text, we find a number of descriptions of the forest that are less concerned with its literal appearance, and more with its spirit. Charles the Wrestler first describes it in 1.1, giving a description which suggests a mystical location – a place of freedom and holiday, in keeping with the notion of Festive comedy:

> CHARLES
> They say he is already in the Forest of Arden,
> and a many merry men with him, and there they live
> like the old Robin Hood of England. They say many
> young gentlemen flock to him every day and fleet the
> time carelessly as they did in the golden world.
>
> (1.1.109–13)

The Golden World or Golden Age was the first of the ages (followed by Silver, Bronze, Heroic and Iron), a period of peace and harmony. The classical Golden Age was often depicted in the European pastoral tradition as a time of rustic innocence, an Arcadia in which nymphs and shepherds lived a simple, idealized life. As we have seen, although when we first encounter the forest it is a threatening and potentially dangerous place, ultimately it proves to be a place of transformation and reconciliation. As Agnes Latham puts it: 'One after another the refugees from the world's unkindness arrive drooping and the forest revives them' (1975: lxx).

The forest is also a place of learning. Duke Senior says of the forest life in 2.1:

> And this our life, exempt from public haunt,
> Finds tongues in trees, books in the running brooks,
> Sermons in stones, and good in everything.
>
> (2.1.15–17)

The notion that humans could learn from nature was common in Renaissance and Medieval literature. Even though, as we hear in Amiens' song 'Blow, blow, thou winter wind', the weather is harsh, it is not as cruel as man's behaviour; his ingratitude, false friendship and foolish love.

> AMIENS
> Blow, blow, thou winter wind,
> Thou art not so unkind
> As man's ingratitude.
> Thy tooth is not so keen
> Because thou art not seen,
> Although thy breath be rude.
> Hey-ho, sing hey-ho, unto the green holly.
> Most friendship is feigning, most loving mere folly.
> Then hey-ho, the holly!
> This life is most jolly.
>
> Freeze, freeze, thou bitter sky,
> That dost not bite so nigh
> As benefits forgot.
> Though thou the waters warp,
> Thy sting is not so sharp
> As friend remembered not.
>
> (2.7.175–90)

These are important tropes in the pastoral tradition, in which nature is viewed as superior and transformative.

Characters

The Elizabethan clown/fool

It is a commonplace, which has some truth in it, to say that Shakespeare's plays feature two distinct kinds of fool or clown figure: the 'natural' clown, a dim-witted figure like Bottom, Dogberry or Costard, prone to malapropisms (the mistaken use of words in place of ones with a similar sound); and the professional fool, for example Feste in *Twelfth Night*, Lear's Fool in *King Lear* and Lavache in *All's Well that Ends Well*. Touchstone falls into this latter category. His milieu is quite clearly the court, and he makes evident his distaste for the country and for the simplicity of its inhabitants, describing them as 'county copulatives' (5.4.55–56) and explicitly distinguishing himself from Corin and William, both of whom he refers to as 'clown' (2.4.63; 5.1.11).

Professional fools or jesters played a key role in medieval and Renaissance households and at court. The role of the professional fool was to provide entertainment and social criticism under the guise of folly. A licensed fool was able to critique his master or other superior household figures without risk of punishment. Touchstone is just such a figure in the court of Duke Frederick. He uses humour to make some serious points; for example in 1.2, when we first encounter him, he engages in some seemingly incomprehensible banter about a knight and some pancakes in order to criticize the lack of honourable behaviour at the court:

> ROSALIND
> Where learned you that oath, fool?
> TOUCHSTONE
> Of a certain knight that swore by his
> honour they were good pancakes, and swore by his
> honour the mustard was naught. Now I'll stand to it:
> the pancakes were naught and the mustard was good,
> and yet was not the knight forsworn.

CELIA
How prove you that in the great heap of your knowledge?
ROSALIND
Ay, marry, now unmuzzle your wisdom.
TOUCHSTONE
Stand you both forth now. Stroke your
chins and swear by your beards that I am a knave.
CELIA
By our beards – if we had them – thou art.
TOUCHSTONE
By my knavery – if I had it – then I were.
But if you swear by that that is not, you are not
forsworn. No more was this knight swearing by his
honour, for he never had any; or if he had, he had sworn
it away before ever he saw those pancakes or that mustard.

(1.2.61–78)

The next few lines have been the subject of textual disagreement. The Folio text reads:

CEL.
Prethee, who is't that thou means't?
CLO.
One that old *Fredericke* your Father loues.
ROS.
My Fathers loue is enough to honor him enough;
speake no more of him, you'l be whipt for taxation one
of these daies.

(F1, TLN. 246–50)

Recognising that Frederick is the name of Celia's father, rather than Rosalind's, most editions simply assign Rosalind's response to Celia. With this emendation, Touchstone's lines seem to be a deliberate criticism of Duke Frederick's corrupt court, implying that the duke's close associate is without honour and is taken as such by Celia. In Polly Findlay's 2016 production at the National Theatre, when Touchstone uttered the line 'One that old Frederick, your father, loves' the surrounding 'court' went quiet, as though his every word was being monitored, Celia's line becoming more a way to placate Frederick's minions than to scold Touchstone.

There has been much discussion in literary criticism and theatre history about the connection between Shakespeare's clowns and fools and the personnel of his acting company, the Lord Chamberlain's Men (later the King's Men). In the early years of the company, its chief comic actor was Will Kemp. Kemp would have played Bottom in *A Midsummer Night's Dream*, Dogberry in *Much Ado About Nothing* and Costard in *Love's Labour's Lost*, amongst other characters. Kemp was a skilled dancer, well known for his jigs, and indeed after he left the company he morris danced from London to Norwich. Kemp is referred to in a play entitled *The Pilgrimage to Parnassus* (1597), where the character Dromo states that 'Clowns have been thrust into plays by head and shoulders ever since Kemp could make a scurvy face' (lines 665–7 quoted in Leishman, 1949). This has been taken to imply that Kemp's was predominantly a physical humour.

Scholars also speculate that Kemp was prone to improvising and that Hamlet's reference to the clown as ambitious inventor of extra lines is a direct reference to Kemp, who had recently left the company:

> HAMLET
> and let those that play
> your clowns speak no more than is set down for them.
> For there be of them that will themselves laugh to set
> on some quantity of barren spectators to laugh too,
> though in the meantime some necessary question of the
> play be then to be considered. – That's villainous and
> shows a most pitiful ambition in the fool that uses it.
>
> (*Ham* 3.2.36–42)

When Kemp left the company in 1599 his place was taken by Robert Armin. Armin was a different kind of actor from Kemp. He was an educated man – a playwright as well as an actor – and was known for his musical abilities. Bart van Es asserts that:

> the impact of Kemp's replacement by Armin is widely acknowledged. Having written a series of clownish roles for Kemp (such as Launcelot Gobbo, Bottom, Peter, and Dogberry) Shakespeare began in 1600 to write a series of very different

characters with an explicitly foolish persona: these included Touchstone, Thersites, Feste, and the Fool in *Lear*. It is near enough certain that all of these roles were crafted specifically for Armin

(2015: 167)

Adding further weight to the argument that Touchstone was a role specifically written for Armin, Andrew Gurr notes the aptness of the name 'Touchstone' for a goldsmith (2004: 218) – Armin had been apprenticed as a goldsmith from 1581 to 1591.

Muriel Bradbrook, in her book *Shakespeare the Craftsman*, describes the way in which these characters are not only different in themselves, but in their relationship with the other characters in the plays: 'The new feature about these parts is that they are dramatically interwoven with the central characters and the central feelings of the play; they demand an actor to play many parts, not just his own brand of clowning' (1969: 50). These roles also demand a commitment to the play and its central story above a selfish desire to entertain. It would be no good if an actor playing Lear's Fool suddenly started improvising. Touchstone is fully integrated into the plot of *As You Like It,* featuring both in the court scenes and those in Arden, and appearing in a number of scenes with Rosalind and Celia, and with Corin, Audrey, William, Jaques and Duke Senior. Touchstone's brand of humour is founded on verbal rather than on physical comedy. His lines are replete with rhetorical devices: puns, elaborate antithesis, synonyms and figures of repetition:

– anaphora (repetition of words at the start of successive clauses):
  In respect that it is solitary, I like it very well;
  but **in respect** that it is private, it is a very vile life.

(3.2.15–16)

– anadiplosis (repetition of the last word or words of one clause at the start of the next):
  Why, if thou never wast at court **thou never sawst good manners**; if **thou never sawst good manners** then thy manners must be **wicked,** and **wickedness** is **sin** and **sin** is damnation.

(3.2.38–41)

- antimetabole (repetition that turns the sentence around)
  'The **fool** doth think he is **wise**, but the **wise**
  man knowns himself to be a **fool**'

(5.1.31–2)

His disquisition on 'The degrees of the lie' in 5.4 is a virtuosic display of verbal dexterity, both for the character and the actor who plays him.

It is, of course, worth noting that Dusinberre argues, contrary to most other critics, that Touchstone was Kemp's role (at least in the first production). For Dusinberre the sequence between Touchstone and Sir Oliver Martext supports this view – 'Kemp's reputation as an anti-Martinist who had many times brought the house down at the Curtain jesting against the Marprelate Puritans would have created instant recognition and mirth in his audience. Here is its favourite comedian with one of his best gags' (2003a: 240). Of course, Dusinberre's theory is firmly tied up with her suppositions about the play's first performance, as discussed in the introduction.

Rosalind and Celia and boy actors on the Renaissance stage

As we have seen with Touchstone, Shakespeare was writing for a company of actors – actors he knew well and could tailor his writing to. This is likely to have also been the case with the characters of Rosalind and Celia. It is well known that female parts on the Renaissance stage were played by boy actors, apprenticed to members of the company, and somewhere in the region of 13 to 21 years of age.

Roland Mushat Frye argues in *Shakespeare: The Art of the Dramatist* that 'Between the theatrical seasons of 1595–96 and 1599–1600 the Chamberlain's Men had two extraordinarily competent boys, one short and the other tall, who could be evidently counted on to act very effectively together' (1982: 49). He is not the first to have suggested this, drawing on evidence from the Middle Comedies – the pairings of Hermia (short and dark) and Helena (tall and blond), Portia and Nerissa, Beatrice and Hero, Viola and Olivia and Rosalind and Celia – all central roles in the plays.

Martin Wiggins provides a more detailed account of the boy players in the company, arguing that the company had four regular boy actors who were cast in order of prominence or seniority. When one boy left the company or graduated to male roles, the next boy would progress up the ladder. Wiggins presents a different picture to Frye – four boys, with different skills, each of whom progressed from minor parts to a leading role. In Wiggins's view Shakespeare is deliberately setting out in *As You Like It* to write a showcase role for one of the boys, possibly in order to allow him to progress to the status of adult actor in the company (2019).

Whether or not the role of Rosalind was specifically tailored to a particular boy, it is certainly tailored to the performance of the role by a boy actor – shown by Shakespeare's use of cross-gendered disguise and deliberately ambiguous references to gender. As discussed in the introduction, it was, perhaps, convenient with boys playing the female roles to have the young actor assume a male persona for part of a play – as do Julia in *Two Gentlemen of Verona,* Viola in *Twelfth Night* and Innogen in *Cymbeline.* But Shakespeare has fun with the metatheatricality of the situation, nowhere more so than in *As You Like It.* From as early as 1.2 Shakespeare begins to play with the audience's knowledge that they are watching two boys playing girls when Touchstone says to Rosalind and Celia:

TOUCHSTONE
Stand you both forth now: stroke your chins, and
swear by your beards that I am a knave.

(1.2.70–1)

Through this line and through Celia's response, 'By our beards, if we had them, thou art' (1.2.72), the audience's attention is drawn to the boy actors beneath the female costumes, who presumably had no beards either, but might expect to get them, unlike their fictional counterparts.

There is some debate as to how Elizabethan audiences would have viewed the boy player, clad as a woman. Some argue that Shakespeare's audiences, accustomed to the convention, would simply have accepted the boy actor as a woman. Others, such as Valerie Traub assert that 'homoeroticism' was a fundamental part of the 'early modern erotic economy', and that plays such as *As You*

Like It provided their Renaissance audiences with 'spectator pleasure' through a 'transgressive glimpse of multiple erotic possibilities' (2001: 135). The case is strengthened with *As You Like It,* through Rosalind's choice of name when in disguise – Ganymede. As mentioned in the introduction, in classical mythology Ganymede was a young shepherd boy, who was abducted by Zeus (or in Roman mythology, Jove) to be his cup-bearer. The word 'ganymede' had, by the Elizabethan period, become slang for a homosexual youth.

That Rosalind, having disguised herself as a man, elects to take on the persona of Orlando's 'very very Rosalind' in 4.1 – such that the Elizabethan audience would have seen a boy, playing a woman, playing a boy, playing a woman – further complicates issues of gender and sexuality in the play. Productions are able to play with this, often to comic effect, with Orlando coming close to kissing Rosalind, or even succumbing to a kiss, only to react in horror when he realises that he has kissed, or nearly kissed, what he thinks is a boy (and indeed would have been a boy on the Renaissance stage).

Finally, in the epilogue to the play, we find the most explicit reference to the boy player beneath the female character. The speech prefix for the epilogue in Act 5 is 'Rosalind', and the speech begins with the actor seemingly in character – 'It is not the fashion to see the lady the epilogue' (Epilogue, 1). This remark refers to the absence of stage epilogues spoken by female characters in earlier Elizabethan plays. However, as the epilogue progresses the layers of identity become increasingly blurred, with the audience invited to acknowledge the presence of the boy player – 'If I were a woman I would kiss as many of you as had beards that pleased me' (Epilogue, 16–18). Brissenden asserts that here 'the actor draws attention to himself as a male more openly than in any other of Shakespeare's plays' (1993: 228). However, the reference may also be seen as a playful comment on Rosalind's assumption of a male disguise in the process of the play. As a 'boy', Rosalind has been liberated; able to assume traditionally masculine qualities – 'I must comfort the weaker vessel, as doublet and hose ought to show itself courageous to petticoat' (2.4.5–7); to engage in sexual banter with Touchstone; and to speak freely to her future husband, tutoring him in the ways of love and marriage. Perhaps she alludes in this comment to a character simultaneously feminine and masculine, straddling gender boundaries and able to tip from one to another, and, as Barbara Hodgdon suggests, in doing so 'acknowledges the erotic ambiguity of gender performances' (2002: 194). Although, as Tiffany Stern has noted, this speech may not have been a permanent part of the play, and rather only performed at a particular performance on the Early Modern stage (2009: 117–19), on the modern stage it is invariably performed and often uncut.

Jaques and the figure of the malcontent

Another character who stems, in part, from Renaissance literary tradition is Jaques. Jaques is entirely Shakespeare's invention and does not feature in the source material. When we are first introduced to the character, in 2.1, it is by the First Lord, who gives him the epithet 'the melancholy Jaques' (2.1.41). In 2.5, Amiens warns him that more singing will make him 'melancholy' and Jaques himself responds:

> I thank it; more, I prithee, more. I can suck
> melancholy out of a song as a weasel sucks eggs.
>
> (2.5.10–11)

He seems to delight in his own misery, and in a form of acerbic, cynical humour, as shown in the final moments of the play when he blesses the marriages of Phoebe and Silvius and Touchstone and Audrey with wry comments on Silvius's sexual desire for Phoebe, and the apparent unsuitability of the match between Touchstone and Audrey:

> JAQUES
> [*to Silvius*] You to a long and well-deserved bed;
> [*to Touchstone*] And you to wrangling, for thy loving
>   voyage
> Is but for two months victualled.
>
> (5.4.188–90)

The Elizabethans understood melancholy according to humourism. They believed that individuals' characters and behaviour were governed by the four humours, determined by different fluids in the human body. An excess of phlegm led to a phlegmatic humour, producing calm; an excess of yellow bile to a choleric humour, producing anger; an excess of blood to a sanguine humour producing bravery; and an excess of black bile to a melancholic humour.

Jaques might be seen as the epitome of the melancholy man, but equally he can be seen as typifying an Elizabethan fashion for deliberately affecting a melancholy pose. Such a pose can be readily associated with the figure of the malcontent, a popular figure in Elizabethan literature. Shakespeare's plays abound with malcontents – figures who often observe the action from the boundaries, expressing discontent at the social structure, politics and behaviour of others. Some, like Hamlet, are sympathetic figures; others, like Iago and Richard III, are villains. Jaques is a cynic. Most malcontents develop some sort of relationship with the audience, mostly through their asides. Although, as discussed in the introduction, asides can be difficult to clearly identify, Jaques has a number of evident asides in 3.3:

- JAQUES *[aside]* O knowledge ill-inhabited, worse than Jove in a thatched house! (8–9)

- JAQUES *[aside]* A material fool. (29)

- JAQUES *[aside]* I would fain see this meeting. (42)

As such, he confides in the audience, sharing his amusement at Touchstone.

Like Marston's malcontent Malevole in his play entitled *The Malcontent* (1604), Jaques takes delight in the clown, and the absurdity of the world as seen through the eyes of a fool. In 2.7 Jaques enters, expressing his pleasure at having met Touchstone: 'A fool, a fool! I met a fool i'th' forest' (2.7.12). He delights in Touchstone's 'rail[ing]' against 'Fortune', his cynical, pessimistic comments:

> And so, from hour to hour, we ripe and ripe,
> And then, from hour to hour, we rot and rot;
>
> (2.7.26–7)

and possibly also in the potential double-entendre of the lines; hour may have been pronounced in Elizabethan England such that it sounded like 'whore', and hence implied the contraction of a venereal disease. Some productions make this double-entendre explicit in Jaques' pronunciation and actions.

In 2.7, Jaques delivers an extended, pessimistic reflection on human existence – 'All the world's a stage' (2.7.140–67). This speech is one of the most famous in the play and has been regularly anthologized and recited out of context, such that one, perhaps, fails to notice how unremittingly negative are the images of the stages of life – the infant 'mewling and puking'; the schoolboy 'whining'; the lover 'sighing'; the soldier seeking pointless honour in the moment of death; the justice fat and 'severe'; the 'pantaloon' shrunken and foolish and finally death.

The speech is, of course, most famous as an extended metatheatrical comment – drawing attention to the 'stage' on which the play is performed, and the 'players' who assume the roles.

Metatheatre

As explored in the introduction, the Elizabethan theatre was inherently metatheatrical in its common use of direct address, asides, overhearings and disguise. *As You Like It* abounds with these features. As discussed above, the language itself often functions to draw our attention directly to the fictional nature of the play – in the explicit references to the boy player performing a female role and in the way in which Corin draws attention to the performative nature of the relationship between Phoebe and Silvius, inviting Rosalind to see 'a pageant truly played' (3.4.48), an invitation to which Rosalind responds with another metatheatrical couplet:

> Bring us to this sight, and you shall say
> I'll prove a busy actor in their play.
>
> (3.4.54–5)

Dusinberre describes Jaques' speech as the 'focal point' in the 'play's self-consciousness about dramatic performance' (2006: 227n), beginning, as it does, with an extended theatrical metaphor:

> All the world's a stage,
> And all the men and women merely players.
> They have their exits and their entrances,
> And one man in his time plays many parts,
> His acts being seven ages.
>
> (2.7.140–4)

In the eighteenth and nineteenth centuries, the speech was often performed as a set piece, with the actor advancing to the footlights to give his well-known, much anticipated oration (Brissenden, 1993: 150).

Both Edzard's and Branagh's films foreground this speech from the outset. Edzard's film begins with James Fox, as Jaques, speaking the lines as a sort of prologue, whilst Branagh's film begins with these words appearing on the screen: 'A dream of Japan / Love and nature in disguise / All the world's a stage'. In 2019 at the RSC, director Kim Sykes used this speech, in particular its opening line, as the inspiration for her production as a whole, particularly the Forest of Arden which became a highly metatheatrical space. The transition into the forest was signalled by a shift into a 'backstage' space, with actors in various states of undress, picking their costumes off a rail and discarding their outfits and wigs from the court as a voice over the tannoy began to make various announcements – 'Miss Stanton to the stage please, Miss Stanton to the stage' (Sophie Stanton being the name of the actress playing Jaques), culminating in the words 'All the world's a stage'. Finally, left alone on the stage, Antony Byrne's Duke Senior raised his arms, bringing up the house lights, which remained on (at various levels) for the remainder of the production, placing the audience and actors in a single democratic space, similar to that of the Elizabethan theatre.

Masque

Another feature of the Renaissance theatre that serves a metatheatrical function and has a discernible impact on the play of *As You Like It* is that of the masque. A masque was an entertainment, usually performed at court, involving singing and dancing, and often designed to celebrate an occasion such as a marriage. It habitually featured gods and goddesses or allegorical figures and magic and was often staged with the use of machinery and spectacle. The masque, though popular in the reign of Elizabeth I, became increasingly so under that of King James (1603–25). We see the influence of this form of entertainment on the marriage sequence in 5.4 of *As You Like It* with the apparent appearance of the god Hymen, accompanied by music. Hymen enters, with Rosalind and Celia (no longer in disguise) to deliver a rather clunky speech, written in mixture of metres. This speech is followed by a series of stylized and patterned utterances from Rosalind, Orlando and Duke Senior and a rather trite trimeter couplet (a pair of rhyming lines each with three metrical feet) from Phoebe:

ROSALIND
[*To Duke Senior*] To you I give myself, for I am yours.
[*To Orlando*] To you I give myself, for I am yours.
DUKE SENIOR
If there be truth in sight, you are my daughter.
ORLANDO
If there be truth in sight, you are my Rosalind.
PHOEBE
If sight and shape be true,
Why then, my love adieu.
ROSALIND
I'll have no father, if you be not he.
I'll have no husband if you be not he.
Nor ne'er wed woman, if you be not she.
(5.4.114–22)

Hymen then launches into a sixteen-line speech, which is followed by a song.

This short sequence has received significant negative attention, with some critics suggesting that it was a later interpolation by someone other than Shakespeare. As Latham notes, such criticism of masque sequences in Shakespeare is common – 'Jupiter on his eagle and the chanting ancestors in *Cymbeline*, the wedding masque in *The Tempest*, and Queen Katharine's vision of angels in *Henry VIII*' (1975: xxi). These moments all seem to jar with our modern theatrical sensibilities. Latham suggests that, 'Readers who reject Shakespearian masques are probably unsympathetic to the masque form as such', disliking its unreality, and most specifically its 'doggerel' (1975: xxiii).

Another reason why critics and theatre practitioners have struggled with this particular masque, and have tried to argue for its later insertion into the play, is that it is something of an anomaly, since the other masques noted above all appear in plays written after 1608, when Shakespeare's company had permanently acquired the indoor Blackfriars Theatre, and in a period when masques had become a particularly fashionable form of entertainment under King James I. In addition, part of the problem with the appearance of Hymen is that there is nothing in the play that seems to anticipate this moment, and the language and stylization seem out of place with the otherwise quite realistic dialogue and characterization that surrounds it.

As was noted in the introduction, modern productions of the play often try to avoid the inclusion of Hymen as a theophany, preferring instead to have one of the other characters in the play assume the role of Hymen for the wedding celebrations. The logic being, perhaps, that if Hymen's rather trite and clunky lines are placed in the mouth of one of the foresters, this excuses their awkwardness and allows the audience to find humour in the clumsy rhymes and metre. Other productions choose to cut the lines altogether. However, some, including Trevor Nunn's 1977 production, have embraced the connection to the Renaissance masque. In Nunn's production, Hymen's entrance was heralded by a thunder-clap, after which he descended from above on a white cloud, accompanied by cherubs, singing in a deliberately Baroque style.

The most recent production of the play at the RSC (Sykes, 2019) was somewhat ambiguous in its treatment of the god, who appeared in the form of a giant puppet, over five metres in height, inspired by the puppets of the French street theatre company Royal de Luxe. Whilst his appearance was described by some as a 'coup-de-theatre' (Tripney, 2019), it was not entirely clear as to whether he was supposed to be viewed by the audience as a puppet, built and manipulated by the people of the forest, or as a god (albeit visibly manipulated by the ensemble of actors). The most plausible explanation in this highly metatheatrical production was that this was a piece of theatrical magic; indeed assistant director Emma Baggott described Hymen, the puppet, in this production as 'a kind of condensed metaphor for the whole production, in that it is an inanimate object that the audience have to imbue with imagination, the puppeteers have to imbue with imagination and movement and care and love and then it comes alive' (Emma Baggot, interview).

Editorial treatment of Hymen has been equally ambivalent over his status as a god or as a person representing a god. The stage direction for Hymen to enter in the Folio text reads simply '*Enter Hymen, Rosalind and Celia*'. Edward Capell, a prominent eighteenth-century Shakespearean critic and editor, was convinced that this was an error on the part of Shakespeare's 'editors', 'who, by bringing in Hymen in *propria persona* [in his own person], make Rosalind a magician indeed; whereas all her conjuration consisted – in fitting up one of the foresters to personate that deity and in putting proper words in his mouth' (1779: 69). Consequently, in *Mr William Shakespeare his Comedies, Histories, and Tragedies* Capell changed the stage direction to read '*Re-enter Rosalind and Celia in their proper Dress, Ros. led by a Person presenting Hymen*' (1767–8: 90), listing this figure in the dramatis personae as 'A person presenting Hymen' (1767: 2). This notion of a person 'presenting' or 'representing' Hymen persisted through numerous editions of the play up until the middle of the twentieth century.

Writing matters

Genre

As You Like It is usually referred to as a comedy or a festive comedy. Consider the various arguments for the description of *As You Like It* as a comedy, a festive comedy or a pastoral comedy. Which do you think is the most appropriate term?

Setting

Imagine that you have been asked to direct a production of *As You Like It*. When and where would you set your production and why? Use specific examples from the text to support your choices.

Metatheatricality

This chapter has discussed some of the metatheatricality in *As You Like It*. Can you identify some more metatheatrical lines or moments in the play?

The Wedding Masque

Do you think that the Wedding Masque works in a modern production? Would you include the figure of Hymen as a god, Hymen played by another character, or would you cut the character all together? Explain your choices.

CHAPTER TWO

Language Forms and Uses

Having explored the literary and theatrical context for the composition of *As You Like It,* we now turn to examine in detail the play's language. This chapter looks at Shakespeare's use of verse and prose in the play and the way in which it moves between the two mediums. It examines the nature of the blank verse and the significance of variations to the iambic pentameter, the use of rhyme and the different registers of prose employed for different characters and situations. It also considers the significance of personal pronouns in the play and the ways in which these can help us to chart the nature and development of the character relationships. The chapter then moves on to examine the theatrical conventions of asides and soliloquies, addressing questions about overhearing (when certain characters overhear the action on stage, unseen by the other characters), audience address (where characters speak directly to the audience) and interiority (when characters express their inner thoughts or feelings). Finally, it tackles various aspects of idiomatic language and rhetoric in the play, including imagery, metaphor and simile, antithesis and wordplay.

Verse and prose

As was noted in the introduction, certain conventions governed the use of verse and prose on the Early Modern stage, with particular characters and situations seeming to lend themselves more obviously to one or the other medium. On the whole, prose was viewed as a lesser medium than verse, used for comic or casual exchanges, whilst verse tended to be used for heightened, serious situations. Dramatic verse was primarily the language of the nobility and prose the language of the lower-class characters. *As You Like It* is written in a mixture of verse and prose, and, like most of Shakespeare's plays, it adheres to some of the conventions. However, by the time that Shakespeare came to write *As You Like It,* he was becoming increasingly flexible in his employment of verse and prose, mixing the two mediums within a single scene and within the language of a particular character. Although the protagonists of *As You Like It* are of a high status – two Dukes and their daughters, and the sons of Sir Rowland de Boys – just over half of *As You Like It* is in prose.

Touchstone, Audrey and William speak almost exclusively in prose, at might befit their class and comic status. The characters who consistently speak in verse are Duke Senior, Phoebe and Silvius (excluding, possibly a few lines of Silvius's in 4.3 which are ambiguous). That the duke speaks in verse befits his status and his age. That Phoebe and Silvius speak in verse might seem contrary to their class and the comic content of many of their lines; however, as we have seen, it is part of the artificiality of the pastoral tradition of which they are a part. Most the rest of the characters in the play: Rosalind, Celia, Orlando, Duke Frederick, Jaques, Oliver, Adam and Corin speak a mixture of verse and prose – depending on the situation and to whom they are talking. As Russ McDonald asserts, in *As You Like It,* much as in *Twelfth Night* and *Much Ado About Nothing,* when it comes to the use of verse and prose, 'theatrical demands tend to overrule the conventions of social class' (2001:114). Prose, for example, suits the casual, witty banter between Rosalind and Celia in 1.2 and 1.3, in spite of the fact that they are both daughters of Dukes:

ROSALIND
    What shall be our sport then?
CELIA
    Let us sit and mock the good housewife Fortune
    From her wheel that her gifts may henceforth be bestowed
      equally.

ROSALIND
I would we could do so, for her benefits are
mightily misplaced – and the bountiful blind women
doth most mistake in her gifts to women.
CELIA
'Tis true, for those that she makes fair she scarce
Makes honest, and those that she makes honest she
Makes very ill-favouredly.

(1.2.30–9)

The percentage of prose in *As You Like It* is roughly 57 per cent. However, the distinction between verse and prose in Shakespeare's work is not always clear-cut. As Dusinberre asserts, '*As You Like It* moves fluidly between prose and verse, and it is often not clear in the Folio which is intended' (2006: 126). One example of such fluidity and uncertainty comes towards the end of 1.2 – just before the moment at which the scene shifts decisively into verse with Duke Frederick's attack on Orlando:

DUKE FREDERICK
I would thou hadst been son to some man else.
The world esteemed thy father honourable,
But I did find him still mine enemy.

(1.2.213–15)

In the Arden Third Series edition, one of the most prominent editions of the play, Dusinberre sets the lines immediately prior to this speech as shared verse, finishing with a single line of prose for Orlando:

DUKE FREDERICK
  No more, no more.
ORLANDO   Yes, I beseech your grace:
  I am not yet well breathed.
DUKE FREDERICK   How dost thou Charles?
LE BEAU
  He cannot speak, my lord.
DUKE FREDERICK   Bear him away.
  What is thy name, young man?

ORLANDO
   Orlando, my liege, the youngest son of Sir
   Rowland be Boys.

(1.2.207–12)

When Giles Block, Head of Text at Shakespeare's Globe theatre, quotes the exchange in his book, *Speaking the Speech* (2013), he sets Orlando's lines as verse, 'Orlando my liege' completing the iambic pentameter begun by the duke's 'What is thy name, young man', something referred to as a 'shared verse line'. Block asserts that 'it's as if the characters have been freed and are now able to express themselves without any concealment . . . at last Orlando can say who he is':

DUKE FREDERICK   Bear him away.
   What is thy name, young man?
ORLANDO   Orlando my liege.
   The youngest son of Sir Rowland de Boys.

(2013: 127)

However, Latham, a previous editor for the Arden Shakespeare, sets the lines as prose, commenting 'It is possible to set all this as blank verse, though the spectators' comments on a wrestling match seem hardly formal enough to warrant it' (1975: 19). Latham's decision seems based less on the rhythmical properties of the lines, and more on her perception of the dramatic function of verse and prose. One might argue that such ambiguous sections (another example occurs at 2.4.158–68) are deliberately thus – suspended somewhere between the conversational mode of prose and the more formal mode of verse – here signalling a transition from the sportive excitement of the wrestling to the realization of Charles' defeat, and leading us into the serious matter of Orlando's disgrace and the first romantic exchange between Orlando and Rosalind.

The question is, why does it matter? For the editor, it matters partly because one has to decide how to set the lines on the page. However, any setting may be accompanied by a note that indicates the ambiguity and explains the editorial thinking behind the lineation. For the actor, it matters because actors and directors view the mediums of verse and prose as distinct and deliberate features of characterization. This can be seen clearly in the quote from Block, above, where he reads into one form of lineation the idea that the move into verse frees the characters to speak their minds. Indeed, Block goes on to analyse what he sees as the metrical structure of Orlando's line, reading into it evidence for the actor about Orlando's relationship with his father, and 'a moment of silence' or 'maybe a silence filled with a gasp' into a missing stress (2013: 127–8). Voice practitioner Patsy Rodenburg states that the use of prose 'by a character or as part of a scene always represents a deliberate choice whose implications need to be fully understood' (2002: 155); Cicely Berry (Voice Director at the RSC from 1969 to 2014) similarly states of verse and prose, 'when you are doing a part which switches between the two, it is important that you mark the changes, and find why the reasoning of the character demands the switch' (1987: 205). Certainly, in many of Shakespeare's plays a move from verse to prose, or vice-versa, marks a significant dramatic shift. Tiffany Stern and Simon Palfrey see such moments, which would have been easily visible to Renaissance actors working from cue parts that contained only their own lines and a brief cue, as 'a visual stage-direction', one of the first things that an actor might have noticed about their role (2007: 332), and hence a significant marker for the development of character.

A particularly noticeable and significant shift from prose to verse comes in 1.3 of *As You Like It*. The scene begins with Rosalind and Celia, alone, exchanging 'jests' (24) about Rosalind's sudden passion for Orlando. Duke Frederick enters, to banish Rosalind from the court, and the whole scene moves into verse.

ROSALIND
   The Duke my father loved his father dearly.
CELIA
   Doth it therefore ensue that you should love his
   son dearly? By this kind of chase I should hate him for
   my father hated his father dearly; yet I hate not
   Orlando.
ROSALIND
   No, faith, hate him not, for my sake.
CELIA
   Why should I not? Doth he not deserve well?

   Enter DUKE [FREDERICK] *with Lords*

ROSALIND
Let me love him for that, and do you love him
because I do. Look, here comes the Duke.
CELIA
With his eyes full of anger.
DUKE FREDERICK
Mistress, dispatch you with your safest haste
And get you from our court.
ROSALIND   Me, uncle?
DUKE FREDERICK   You, cousin.
(1.3.28–39)

Margery Garber suggests that 'the shift from prose to verse ... underscores the sudden change from intimacy to formality' (1986: 105). Garber's comment is in keeping with common perceptions of the function of verse and prose and makes perfect sense. Rosalind and Celia are essentially engaging in some intimate gossip, before the duke enters, with his lords, shifting the scene into the more formal, public sphere. However, directors Peter Hall and Giles Block read the significance of a move from verse to prose somewhat differently. For Hall, 'there is always a deliberate formality about the prose; it is more self-conscious than verse' (2003:43). Hall states that whilst 'the verse represents ordinary speech, the prose stands for heightened speech' (2003: 43). Initially, Hall's statement seems in direct contradiction to those of most commentators; however, when discussing the transition from prose to verse in 1.5 of *Twelfth Night,* he comments 'verse is about feeling and anguish leading to protest; prose is about reason, argument and wit' (2003: 117). Here we see a similarity with Block's assertion, that prose is a medium of concealment, a medium which provides the 'surface' that 'covers ... what is really going on beneath' (2013: 126). Both Hall and Block see prose as something constructed and artificial, whilst verse is the medium of free speech, of revelation of true feelings.

These different perspectives on the function of prose have quite different implications for a reading of this scene, and, in particular, the role of Rosalind. If we take Garber's view, Duke Frederick interrupts the women's informal, playful conversation, using formal, dismissive terms. Rosalind immediately adjusts to the formality, choosing her words carefully and containing any anger and distress she is feeling, through her dignified speech. Block and Hall's analysis would seem to suggest almost the reverse, that Rosalind's response is a genuine revelation of her true feelings – a straightforward, heartfelt declaration of the truth of her situation, 'Never so much as in a thought unborn / Did I offend your highness' (1.3.48–9), delivered without the 'gloss' of prose. Both are viable interpretations; both can be played convincingly on stage.

Whichever way we choose to interpret the movement from prose to verse or verse to prose, one thing is certain: in order for a dramatic shift to effectively occur, the distinction between verse and prose must be apparent to the audience as well as the actor. In the modern theatre there is a danger that such a distinction can be elided, with some actors having a tendency to break up the verse lines with the aim of making them sound as natural and real as possible. However, we can be fairly certain that the difference between verse and prose would have been audible, and recognizable to an Elizabethan audience, as is evidenced by this brief exchange from *As You Like It*:

JAQUES
    Yes, I have gained my experience.

Enter ORLANDO

ROSALIND
    And your experience makes you sad. I had
    rather have a fool to make me merry than experience to
    make me sad – and to travel for it too.
ORLANDO
    Good day and happiness, dear Rosalind.
JAQUES
    Nay then, God b'wi' you an you talk in blank verse.

(4.1.23–9)

Rosalind and Jaques have been conversing with one another in prose, when Orlando enters with a perfectly regular line of iambic pentameter. In order for Jaques' subsequent jibe to work, the audience must recognise the difference between the two mediums as well as their common conventions, namely the status of verse as the heightened language of the lover.

The registers of prose

As we have already seen, it is dangerous to generalize about the nature of the language used in verse and prose, particularly in the plays written after around 1595, partly because of the different registers of prose that Shakespeare employs. Whilst we might be tempted to think of prose as akin to everyday speech, there is a significant difference between the scenes in which characters go about their everyday business, conversing in straightforward prose, and the myriad of more complex, striking uses to which prose is put in the plays. Here we can see a parallel between Shakespeare and John Lyly, the prominent novelist and dramatist whose work had a profound influence on Shakespeare. If we look at Lyly's play *Campaspe,* for example, we can see a keen distinction between the language of Hephestion, the General of Alexander the Great's army, and that of the servants of Diogenes. Here is Hephestion:

> HEPHESTION
> I cannot tell, *Alexander*, whether the report be more shameful to be heard, or the cause sorrowful to be believed? What is the son of *Philip,* king of Macedon become the subject of *Campaspe*, the captive of *Thebes*? Is that mind, whose greatness the world could not contain, drawn within the compass of an idle alluring eye? Will you handle the spindle with *Hercules*, when you should shake the spear with *Achilles*? Is the warlike sound of drum & trump turned to the soft noise of lyre & lute, the neighing of barbed steeds, whose loudness filled the air with terror, and whose breathes dimmed the sun with smoke, converted to delicate tunes and amorous glances?
>
> (*Campaspe,* 2.2)

This speech is packed with rhetorical devices, most notably those of antithesis and the rhetorical question (a question designed to make a statement or produce an effect or rather than to elicit an answer). Here, by contrast we see the servants in conversation, where the language is simple and unembellished:

PSYLLUS
Behold *Manes* where thy master is, seeking either for bones for his dinner, or pins for his sleeves. I will go salute him.
MANES
Do so, but mum not a word that you saw *Manes*.
GRANICHUS
Then stay thou behind, and I will go with *Psyllus*.

[MANES *stands apart.*]

PSYLLUS
All hail *Diogenes* to your proper person.
(*Campaspe*, 2.1)

There are similar distinctions in Shakespeare's prose in *As You Like It*. We find, for example, this simple prose conversation:

WILLIAM
Good ev'n, Audrey.
AUDREY
God ye good ev'n, William.
WILLIAM
And good ev'n to you, sir.
TOUCHSTONE
Good ev'n, gentle friend. Cover thy head, cover thy head. Nay, prithee be covered. How old are you, friend?
WILLIAM
Five-and-twenty, sir.
TOUCHSTONE
A ripe age. Is thy name William?
WILLIAM
William, sir.
TOUCHSTONE
A fair name. Wast born i'th' forest here?
WILLIAM
Ay, sir, I thank God.
TOUCHSTONE
'Thank God' – a good answer. Art rich?

WILLIAM
  Faith, sir, so-so.

(5.1.14–26)

This is an exchange between Audrey, a goatherd; William, a country youth; and Touchstone, the clown. One might expect all of these characters to speak in prose, due to their social status and comic function. Audrey, as is established at her first entrance in 3.3, is uneducated, struggling to understand some of Touchstone's more involved wordplay and literary references – 'I do not know what poetical is' (3.3.15). Her utterances in 3.3 are mostly in plain, simple, direct language, and this pattern continues into 5.1. William appears only in 5.1, where he is referred to, by Touchstone, as a 'clown' (5.1.11) in the sense of 'country bumpkin' (Greenblatt et al., 1997: 1647). His prose utterances are all between two and seven words in length and are simple, unadorned answers to Touchstone's questions. Touchstone's language, though almost exclusively prose, is – for the most part – rhetorically complex. However, in the passage in 5.1, he begins by deliberately adjusting his language to the level of those with whom he is conversing in a way that could certainly be played as overtly patronizing. However, if we continue to explore the scene we see that Touchstone's prose becomes increasingly convoluted; full of aphorisms (pithy expressions of truth) – 'to have is to have'; references to rhetorical devices – 'it is a figure in rhetoric' (meaning a rhetorical commonplace); and Latin terms – *ipse* (translated as 'he himself'):

TOUCHSTONE
  Then learn this of me: to have is to have.
  For it is a figure in rhetoric that drink, being poured out of a cup into a glass, by filling the one doth empty the other. For all your writers do consent that *ipse* is 'he'.
  Now you are not *ipse*, for I am he.

(5.1.40–4)

His dialogue with William finally culminates in an elaborate invective which follows the rules of rhetoric and grammar in its construction:

TOUCHSTONE
He, sir, that must marry this woman.
Therefore, you clown, abandon (which is, in the
vulgar, 'leave') the society (which in the boorish is
'company') of this female (which in the common is
'woman'); which together is 'abandon the society of
this female', or clown, thou perishes! Or to thy better
understanding, diest. Or (to wit) I kill thee, make thee
away, translate they life into death, thy liberty into
bondage. I will deal in poison with thee, or in bastinado
or in steel. I will bandy with thee in faction; I will
o'errun thee with policy. I will kill thee a hundred and
fifty ways! Therefore tremble and depart.

(5.1.46–57)

This is highly patterned, self-conscious prose which is full of devices of repetition, most notably anaphora (the repetition of words at the beginning of successive clauses) – 'which ... which ... which ... which', 'Or ... Or', 'I will ... I will ... I will ... I will'; hyperbole (excessive exaggeration) – 'I will kill thee a hundred and fifty ways'; and patterning, with the repeated use of the rhetorical 'rule of three' (a rule expounded in rhetorical handbooks, by which the speaker is advised to illustrate each point with three instances) – 'Or (to wit) I kill thee, make thee away, translate thy life into death'.

Touchstone is not the only character to use such heightened rhetorical prose. Indeed, Brian Vickers states of *As You Like It* that 'no other play contains as many witty set-speeches ... and in no other play are logic and rhetorical used so brilliantly, albeit also as static solo performances' (1985: 200). Rosalind and Celia also function brilliantly as a double-act in this respect, particularly when we first encounter them in 1.2, punning on the roles of Nature and Fortune (30–54), bantering with Touchstone (55–89) and mocking Le Beau (90–136). However, it is once Rosalind encounters Orlando in the forest that she truly begins to indulge in patterned set-pieces. Whilst Vickers asserts that in Shakespeare's plays 'no serious love affairs are conducted or concluded in prose' (1985: 389–90), Rosalind's wooing of Orlando is not, at least superficially, in earnest, and both the long scenes (3.2 and 4.1) in which – disguised as Ganymede – she seeks to tutor Orlando in the ways of love and marriage are entirely in prose. One could take almost any of

Rosalind's lengthy speeches in 3.2 and find multiple rhetorical tropes and figures (as will be done below). For now, we turn to the play's verse.

Blank verse and its variations

As was established in the introduction, the main verse form used by Shakespeare in his plays is blank verse – a line of verse consisting of five iambic feet. Much of the verse of *As You Like It* is formed of regular lines of iambic pentameter:

> DUKE FREDERICK
> I would thou hadst been son to some man else.
>
> (1.2.213)

Feminine endings

The most common variation to this pattern is what has traditionally been known as a 'feminine' ending. Given the negative gender implications of this term, some prefer to use the terms 'weak ending' or 'extra-syllable ending'. The feminine ending can have a number of different effects depending on its context within a speech. George T. Wright suggests that the feminine ending may make 'blank verse seem more speechlike, *less* patterned' and that when blank verse which 'regularly ends with an unstressed syllable takes on a quality which, in different lines, may variously be described as soft, haunting, yearning, pliant, seductive' (1988: 162, 164). An example of a more 'speechlike' quality may be found in Corin's speech to Rosalind, Celia and Touchstone in 2.4:

> My master is of churlish disposition   FEMININE
> And little recks to find the way to heaven FEMININE
> By doing deeds of hospitality.
>
> (2.4.74–6)

Here, the feminine endings combine with the enjambment (the sense flowing over the ends of the verse lines) to give a conversational quality to Corin's lines.

The quality of 'yearning' may be found most obviously in 5.2, in the sequence where various characters yearn for their loves. Here is Silvius, speaking of his longing for Phoebe:

SILVIUS
  It is to be all made of fantasy
  All made of passion, and all made of wishes   FEMININE
  All adoration, duty and observance   FEMININE
  All humbleness, all patience and impatience   FEMININE
  All purity, all trial, all obedience   FEMININE
                                                                (5.2.90–5)

A few lines later, Phoebe, Silvius and Orlando repeat the same phrase, with a feminine ending:

PHOEBE
  If this be so, why blame you me to love you?
SILVIUS
  If this be so, why blame you me to love you?
ORLANDO
  If this be so, why blame you me to love you?
                                                               (5.2.99–101)

These lines may be described as yearning; they are also questions. The feminine ending, with its upward impulse (a final light syllable) can be seen to have a questioning quality. One of the most famous of Shakespeare's speeches, in which a character is questioning his very existence, begins with four lines with feminine endings:

HAMLET   To be, or not to be – that is the
    question   FEMININE
  Whether 'tis nobler in the mind to suffer   FEMININE
  The slings and arrows of outrageous fortune   FEMININE
  Or to take arms against a sea of troubles   FEMININE
  And by opposing end them; . . .
                                                             (*Ham.* 3.1.55–9)

Other metrical feet

As Shakespeare's career progressed, he increasingly introduced alternative metrical feet (the repeated unit of the verse that is made up of stressed and unstressed syllables) into his verse lines. These alternative feet break up the monotony of regular iambic lines and allow more freedom to the verse. They also have a dramatic function. Other than the iamb (unstressed followed by stressed – u /), the most common metrical feet used by Shakespeare are:

- The anapaest – two unstressed syllables followed by a stressed syllable: u u /
- The trochee – a stressed syllable followed by an unstressed syllable (the reverse of an iamb): / u
- The spondee – two stressed syllables: / /

Anapaests are a regular feature of Shakespeare's verse, permitting a more conversational style by admitting extra syllables into a line. Anapaests often occur when characters have a lot to say – as if they need the extra syllables to get everything in. One of the best examples of the use of anapaests in *As You Like It* comes in Rosalind's invective to Phoebe in 3.5. Rosalind, disguised as Ganymede, steps in to interfere in the exchange between Phoebe and Silvius:

ROSALIND
   And why, I pray you? Who might be
      your mother,   FEMININE
   That you insult, exult, and all at once
                        u   u /   anapaest
   Over the wretched? What [though you have]
      no beauty –   FEMININE
[. . .]
   I see no more in you than in the
      ordinary   TRIPLE
                                                ENDING
[. . .]
   That can entame my spirits to your worship   FEMININE
               u   u   /   u   u /   anapaests
   You foolish shep[herd, wherefore] [do you foll]ow her

LANGUAGE: FORMS AND USES

>   Like foggy south, puffing with wind and rain?
>   u u /   anapaest
>   You are a thousand times a prop[erer man]
>   Than she a woman. 'Tis such fools as you
>   That make the world full of ill-favoured children FEMININE
>   'Tis not her glass but you that flatters her,
>   And out of you she sees herself more proper   FEMININE
>   uu/   anapaest
>   Than any of her lin[eaments] can show her.   FEMININE
>   But, mistress, know yourself; down on your knees,
>   u   u   /   anapaest
>   And thank [heaven fas]ting for a good man's love
>   For I must tell you friendly in your ear:
>   Sell when you can, you are not for all markets. FEMININE
>   Cry the man mercy, love him, take his offer   FEMININE
>   u u /   anapaest
>   Foul is most foul, [being foul] to be a scoffer FEMININE
>   (3.5.36–63)

The series of anapaests combines with a number of feminine endings, and what are known as triple-endings (where the line ends with two additional unstressed syllables). Rosalind is clearly exercised and passionate in her desire to resolve Phoebe and Silvius's love problems, which is evident in the way in which the extra syllables come thick and fast.

When a line begins with the trochee or a spondee, it often has the effect of grabbing the attention of the audience or the other characters. When Duke Frederick bursts into 1.2, banishing Rosalind, he begins his speech forcefully with a trochee:

>   /   u
>   [Mistress], dispatch you with your safest haste
>   And get you from our court.
>   (1.2.38–9)

When Duke Senior begins his address to his 'brothers and co-mates' he captures their attention with a trochee:

/ u
[Now, my] co-mates and brothers in exile

(2.1.1)

His speech, a public oration in which he attempts to cajole his followers into appreciation of their surroundings, has a series of lines which seem to begin with either a trochee or a spondee:

DUKE SENIOR
  Now, my co-mates and brothers in exile,
  Hath not old custom made our life more sweet
  Than that of painted pomp? Are not these woods
  More free from peril than the envious court?

(2.1.1–4)

Lines 2 and 4 might be said to begin with spondees, since both 'Hath' and 'not' and 'More' and 'free' seem to demand stress. The additional stresses at the beginning of lines suggest that the speaker is working hard to reinforce their words; to persuade their listeners. It is worth saying at this point that the presence of particular metrical feet is often subjective and dependent on how one chooses to stress certain words in a line. However, monosyllabic words often seem to invite stress, as is the case here.

Monosyllabic lines

This leads us neatly to the monosyllable, and the presence and dramatic function of monosyllabic lines. Monosyllabic lines abound in Shakespeare's plays, some of the most famous being:

ANTONIO
  In sooth I know not why I am so sad.

(*Merchant of Venice*, 1.1.1)

OTHELLO
  It is the cause, it is the cause my soul.

(*Othello*, 5.2.1)

These are key moments in the plays; points at which the characters are searching their souls. The monosyllabic nature of the line throws a stress onto each word, making it emphatic. John Barton describes monosyllabic lines as 'one of the most important ingredients in Shakespeare's poetry', suggesting that Shakespeare uses monosyllabic lines 'for particularly charged or heightened moments' (1984: 196–7). He informs actors that such lines cannot be rushed, encouraging them to speak them slowly so that each word can 'breathe' (1984: 98).

Monosyllabic lines occur a number of times in *As You Like It*, and, as Barton suggests, often at moments of high emotion. Duke Frederick's first line to Orlando, at the moment that the play first moves decisively into verse, is a line of monosyllables:

DUKE FREDERICK
   I wouldst thou hadst been son to some man else.

(1.2.213)

The Duke speaks plainly, and emphatically. When, in this next scene he banishes Rosalind, it is with a monosyllabic half-line, similarly plain and emphatic:

DUKE FREDERICK
   And get you from our court.

(1.3.39)

A high number of monosyllables occur in 3.5 in the scene where Rosalind (as Ganymede) and Celia (as Aliena) go with Corin to eavesdrop on the conversation between Phoebe and Silvius. At this point Phoebe is scorning Silvius; rejecting his advances. Her first speech is replete with monosyllabic lines, all of which seem designed to press home to Silvius her disdain for him:

PHOEBE   [. . .]
   Now I do frown on thee with all my heart,
   And if mine eyes can wound, now let them kill thee.
   [. . .]
   Or if thou canst not – O, for shame, for shame –
   [. . .]
   Now show the wound mine eye hath made in thee.
   [. . .]
   Some scar of it; lean thou upon a rush,

[...]
Nor I am sure there is no force in eyes
That can do hurt.

(3.5.15–27)

Rosalind (as Ganymede) is equally emphatic in her rejection of Phoebe, once it dawns on her that Phoebe is falling in love with her:

> ROSALIND
> Why what means this? Why do you look on me?
>
> (3.5.42)

> ROSALIND
> I pray you do not fall in love with me,
>
> (3.5.81)

There are many more instances in the play of the use of monosyllabic lines used for of emphatic statements or aphorisms, as well as by characters suddenly thrown by a situation – hesitant in their responses.

Other metres

Whilst most of the verse in *As You Like It* takes the form of iambic pentameter (with occasional metrical variations, as noted above) there are a few passages that make use of different metres. The first of these comes in 2.4, the first time that we encounter Silvius:

> SILVIUS
> O, thou didst then never love so heartily!
> If thou rememb'rest not the slightest folly
> That ever love did make thee run into,
> Thou hast not loved.
> Or if thou hast not sat as I do now,
> Wearying thy hearer in thy mistress' praise,
> Thou hast not loved.
> Or if thou hast not broke from company

Abruptly, as my passion now makes me,
Thou hast not loved.
O Phoebe, Phoebe, Phoebe!

(2.4.30–40)

Here, Silvius's iambic lines are interspersed with the short line 'Thou hast not loved', a line of iambic dimeter (two iambic feet – u / u /). Dusinberre notes that this repeated short line 'acts as a refrain, as in shepherds' pastoral songs' (2006: 205). This, of course, fits with the notion of Silvius as a stock pastoral figure.

In discussing the pastoral conventions of the play, Chapter 1 also noted the artificial, song-like verse of 5.2, with the repetition of:

SILVIUS
And so am I for Phoebe.
PHOEBE
And I for Ganymede.
ORLANDO
And I for Rosalind.
ROSALIND
And I for no woman.

(5.2.81–4)

Once again, a different metre is introduced; here an iambic trimeter (three iambic feet), with Silvius's line having a feminine ending. Jonathan P. Lamb describes this patterned verse as 'a pastoral eclogue, of the sort that occurs throughout Sidney's *Arcadia* and other pastoral romances of the 1590s' (2017: 137).

Having hankered after Ganymede, when Phoebe discovers that the object of her infatuation is, in fact, a woman, iambic trimeter is also, appropriately, the metre that she uses to bid her farewell:

PHOEBE
If sight and shape be true,
Why then, my love adieu.

(5.4.18–19)

Having identified lines of dimeter (two metrical feet) and trimeter (three metrical feet) in the play, we now move to tetrameter, a line of four metrical feet. Tetrameter is the metre used by Orlando for his love poetry written to Rosalind, and, in a neat parallel, by Phoebe when writing her love letter to Ganymede. The metre is mostly catalectic trochaic tetrameter – a series of four trochees, with the final unstressed syllable missing in most lines (/u /u /u /), with some lines of iambic tetrameter. We hear two of Orlando's poems in 3.2 – the first read by Rosalind and the second by Celia; both are intentionally bad and over-written:

ROSALIND
From the east to western Inde,
No jewel is like Rosalind.
Her worth, being mounted on the wind,
Through all the world bears Rosalind.
All the pictures fairest lined
Are but black to Rosalind.
Let no fair be kept in mind
But the fair of Rosalind.

(3.2.85–92)

In this poem, each pair of lines is heavily end-stopped on the name 'Rosalind'. When the modern edited text is spoken aloud in modern English pronunciation, the first two rhymes work, whilst the second two render Rosalind's name akin to 'Rosalinde', something which is often played up on the contemporary stage, with Rosalind reacting with disdain or disappointment at Orlando's failure to get her name right. However, when Shakespeare rhymes the word 'wind' elsewhere in the canon, it is with words like 'unkind', 'behind', 'mind' and 'find', and, indeed, the way in which the poem is printed in the Folio text suggests a series of rhymes, with Rosalind's name pronounced Rosalinde throughout:

ROS. *From the east to westerne Inde,*
no iewel is like Rosalinde,
Hir worth being mounted on the winde,
through all the world beares Rosalinde.
All the pictures fairest Linde,
are but blacke to Rosalinde:

Let no face bee kept in mind,
but the faire of Rosalinde.

(F1, TLN.1286–1293)

It has been suggested that this is the way in which the name would have been spoken in Elizabethan pronunciation, and, therefore, throughout the play. Thus, when Touchstone reacts by ridiculing the poem, his criticism may be more for the laboured verse and repetitive rhyme scheme than for the poem's failure to rhyme:

TOUCHSTONE
I'll rhyme you so eight years together, dinners and
suppers and sleeping-hours excepted: it is the
right butter-women's rank to market.

(3.2.93–5)

Indeed, he compares the poem's style to the sorts of chants uttered by groups of dairywomen on their way to market, before aping the poem with increasingly coarse allusions.

The second poem is written in the same metre, but with a different rhyme scheme of alternate rhyming lines. It is packed with references to classical figures, with whom Orlando compares his 'Rosalinda' (134). It is also full of unbearably clunky lines with awkward syntax:

CELIA
Why should this a desert be?
For it is unpeopled? No:

(3.2.132–3)

It also collapses metrically in its final couplet, with a nine-syllable line followed by an eight-syllable one. Here, again, modern pronunciation also means that the rhyme collapses; a gift for the actor playing Celia (although 'have' and 'slave' would probably have rhymed in Elizabethan pronunciation; see Crystal, 2016):

Heaven would that she these gifts should have,
And I to live and die her slave.

(3.2.150–1)

Shakespeare most commonly uses catalectic trochaic tetrameter as the metre of the supernatural – the witches in *Macbeth* and the fairies in *A Midsummer Night's Dream*. However, as Marina Tarlinskaja shows in her study *Shakespeare and the Versification of English Drama, 1561–1642*, in English verse, iambic and trochaic tetrameters had 'developed different thematic preferences', the trochee being more associated with a 'rural setting' and with 'villagers, shepherds and shepherdesses' (2014: 269). Thus, the dominant metre of Orlando's poetry, and that of Phoebe's, might be seen to fit with the play's pastoral theme. That Phoebe's letter to Rosalind as Ganymede is rather better than Orlando's offerings also fits with the notion of her character as a construct of the pastoral ideal – now she has become the scorned Petrarchan lover, writing love poetry to the object of her affection. It is also worth noting that the poems that Rosader (Orlando) sends to Rosalynde in Lodge's poem are written in tetrameter, and thus, Shakespeare might also seem to be following his source in the use of this metre:

> ROSALYNDES DESCRIPTION
> *Like to the clear in highest sphere*
> *Where all imperial glory shines,*
> *Of self same colour is her hair*
> *Whether unfolded or in twines:*
> *Heigh ho, fair* Rosalynde.
>
> (Lodge, 1590: H4v, spelling modernized)

Chapter 1 has already touched on the figure of Hymen, who appears in 5.4. speaking in a range of metres. Hymen's first speech begins in iambic trimeter – a rhyming couplet, both lines with feminine endings. They are followed by a line of five syllables:

> HYMEN
>   Then is there mirth in heaven
>   When earthly things made even
>   Atone together.
>
> (5.4.106–8)

This same pattern in repeated and then followed by a pair of rhyming iambic tetrameter lines:

Good Duke, receive thy daughter.
Hymen from heaven brought her,
Yea brought her hither,
That thou mightst join her hand with his
Whose heart within his bosom is.

(5.4.109–13)

The verse is clunky – even allowing for differences in pronunciation which might have made 'heaven' rhyme with 'even'. There are awkward inversions of syntax – 'Whose heart within his bosom is'; forced rhymes, such as 'daughter' and 'brought her' and excessive alliteration – 'O blessed bond of board and bed'. Hymen then launches into a sixteen-line speech beginning in iambic trimeter:

Peace, ho. I bar confusion.
'Tis I must make conclusion.
Of these most strange events.
Here's eight that must take hands
To join in Hymen's bands,
If truth holds true contents.

(5.4.123–8)

The speech then moves into rhyming trochaic tetrameter (some catalectic – missing the last beat in the line). The whole speech is doggerel-like, with an incessant sing-song quality.

Rhyme

This brings us neatly to the topic of rhyme in the play. We have seen here a series of poems and speeches with different rhyme schemes – some alternating rhymes, some rhyming couplets and some AAB BBC:

Why should this a desert be,	A
For it is unpeopled? No!	B
Tongues I'll hang on every tree	A
That shall civil sayings show:	B

(3.2.122–5)

From the east to western Inde,
No jewel is like Rosalind.

(3.2.85–6)

Peace, ho. I bar confusion.	A
'Tis I must make conclusion.	A
Of these most strange events.	B
Here's eight that must take hands	C
To join in Hymen's bands,	C
If truth holds true contents.	B

(5.4.123–8)

I have indicated here how these rhyme schemes might be represented, the first as ABAB, and the third as AAB CCB. These rhyme schemes refer to the final sound in each of the lines – the first being given the designation A, the next B and so forth. The rhyming schemes combine with the metre of these pieces to further enhance their 'sing-song' quality.

With the exception of poems and speeches such as Hymen's, the use of rhyme in Shakespeare's work is otherwise mostly restricted to rhyming couplets. It is commonly asserted that Shakespeare frequently used rhyming couplets at the end of scenes. This is certainly true of his earlier plays. In *The Comedy of Errors* (*c.*1592), for example, eight of the eleven scenes end in a rhyming couplet, and one in a near-rhyme. However, the practice becomes far less common in his later work. In *As You Like It,* being somewhere in the middle of the canon, of the twenty-two scenes plus Epilogue, eight end in a rhyming couplet, for example:

After my flight. Now go we in content
To liberty and not to banishment.

(1.3.134–5)

The end of 1.2 has a rather more interesting style of ending, which becomes increasingly common in Shakespeare's later work. Here we get the rhyming couplet that we have come to expect at the end of a scene, but this is then followed by a short verse line:

Thus must I from the smoke into the smother,

> From tyrant Duke unto a tyrant brother.
> But heavenly Rosalind!
>
> (1.2.276–9)

It is as if, following his decisive couplet, Orlando cannot but help exclaim at his new-found love, with the exclamation 'But heavenly Rosalind' falling outside the metrical structure.

As well as occurring at the ends of scenes, Shakespeare sometimes uses rhyming couplets at the end of speeches, where they serve a similar function of summing up the action:

> CORIN
>   there is nothing
> That you will feed on. But what is come see,
> And in my voice most welcome shall you be.
>
> (2.4.84–6)

It is as if, for Corin this feels like the end of the conversation, but Rosalind (as Ganymede) has another question, leading to further dialogue before Corin rounds-off the scene with a similar couplet:

> I will your very faithful feeder be,
> And buy it with your gold right suddenly.
>
> (2.4.98–9)

Shakespeare also uses rhyming couplets to reinforce; sometimes rhyming couplets are used for aphorisms or pithy expressions: 'Foul is most foul, being foul to be a scoffer', 'Whoever loved that loved not at first sight', including comic ones such as Touchstone's 'We must be married, or we must live in bawdry':

> ROSALIND
> Cry the man mercy, love him, take his offer;
> Foul is most foul, being foul to be a scoffer.
>
> (3.5.62–3)

> PHOEBE
> Dead shepherd, now I find thy saw of might:
> 'Who ever loved, that loved not at first sight?'
>
> (3.5.82–3)

TOUCHSTONE   Come sweet Audrey,
   We must be married, or we must live in bawdry
                                              (3.3.88–9)

A particularly striking use of rhyme comes at the beginning of 3.2, where we find Orlando, running through the forest pinning his verses of love on the trees. Orlando delivers a ten-line speech (a dizain), with the rhyme scheme ABAB, CDCD EE – two quatrains (four lines of alternating rhyme) and a rhyming couplet:

Hang there, my verse, in witness of my love.	A
And thou, thrice-crowned queen of night, survey	B
With thy chaste eye, from thy pale sphere above,	A
Thy huntress' name that my full life doth sway.	B
O Rosalind, these trees shall be my books,	C
And in their barks my thoughts I'll character,	D
That every eye which in this forest looks	C
Shall see thy virtue witnessed everywhere	D
Run, run, Orlando, carve on every tree	E
The fair, the chaste and unexpressive she!	E

                                              (3.2.1–10)

The rhyme scheme is reminiscent of that of a sonnet, which consists of three quatrains and a couplet, and is a form closely associated with love poetry. One might note that Shakespeare uses the embedded sonnet elsewhere in his works; Romeo and Juliet's meeting in 1.5 (lines 92–105) is perhaps the most famous of these, and is another passage of intense love.

The songs

As You Like It has the most songs of any Shakespeare play – five in total: 'Under the Greenwood Tree' (2.5), 'Blow, blow, thou winter wind' (2.7), 'What shall he have that killed the deer?' (4.2), 'It was a lover and his lass' (5.3) and 'Wedding is great Juno's crown' (5.4). These are written in a mixture of metres. The preponderance of songs in the play may be partly due to the influence of the pastoral genre on its composition. Lodge's *Rosalynde,* the play's main source, contains a number of songs. As with many of the songs that occur in Shakespeare's work, it seems that at least some of those in *As You Like It* were in circulation prior to the play's composition. Shakespeare, like many writers today, seems to have inserted well-known songs, or tunes for which he may have composed new lyrics, into his plays. 'What shall he have that killed the deer' appears as a round for four voices in John Hilton's *Catch that Catch Can* (1652), but was probably written well before its publication, and an alternative text of 'It was a lover and his lass' was published in Thomas Morley's *First Book of Airs* (1600). There is no extant contemporary music for the other three songs, although this doesn't necessarily mean that they were original compositions for the play.

Personal pronouns

Modern English has only one second person pronoun: you. Elizabethan English had two – you and thou. Either of these pronouns could be used to address someone in the singular, but the ways in which they were used had significant implications in terms of status and relationships; as significant as the name or title by which someone was addressed. As Penelope Freedman details in *Power and Passion in Shakespeare's Pronouns*, 'for a modern Anglophone audience, as indeed for most actors and directors, the distinction between "you" and "thou" is virtually lost' (2007: 1); however, it is vital to an understanding of how character relationships function in Shakespeare's plays. The use of 'you' and 'thou' and their attendant forms in Elizabethan English: your and yours (for you) and thee, thy, thine (for thou) resembled the use of *vous* and *tu* in French. 'You', like *vous*, was both the plural and the respectful form of address and was the common pronoun of address. 'Thou', like *tu*, was the intimate form of address, used to indicate a particular closeness. It was also the patronising form used address to social inferiors, and the disrespectful form used to express anger or to insult someone.

Throughout *As You Like It*, much as with the movements between verse and prose, it is the shifts from one pronoun to another that are often of most interest. One such example occurs in 1.3 when Duke Frederick appears to banish Rosalind. On his entrance, the duke addresses Rosalind with the pronoun 'you', indicating a degree of formality but also of distance:

> DUKE FREDERICK
> Mistress, dispatch you with your safest haste
> And get you from our court.
>
> (1.3.38–9)

Rosalind, as might be expected, addresses her uncle and superior with a respectful 'your':

> ROSALIND   I do beseech your grace,
>
> (1.3.42)

However, after her calm defence, the duke suddenly switches to the 'thou' form:

> DUKE FREDERICK   . . .
> Let it suffice thee that I trust thee not.
>
> (1.3.52)

The change in pronoun indicates a change in tone, from a degree of measured formality to something more vicious and direct.

Some of the most interesting relationships to explore in terms of the use of personal pronouns are those of the pairs of lovers in the play. One might expect lovers to use the intimate pronoun 'thou' to one another; however, Elizabethan social conventions were slightly more nuanced. Whilst lovers might use the pronoun 'thou' to express their reciprocal love, it was not appropriate for women to use this pronoun until it had first been used by the man. Thus the women in Shakespeare's plays who initiate the use of 'thou' do so inappropriately – Goneril and Regan to Edmund (in *King Lear*), Olivia to Cesario (in *Twelfth Night*) and Titania to Bottom (in *A Midsummer Night's Dream*). Phoebe is another female character who uses 'thou' to a male lover (Silvius) who uses 'you'. However, this is not as a forward indication of her love, but of her distain, and sometimes pity, at least until her final lines, which may be delivered as a change of heart, or as a grudging acceptance of her situation:

> PHOEBE
> I will not eat my word, now thou art mine,
> Thy faith my fancy to thee doth combine.
>
> (5.4.147–8)

Touchstone and Audrey are seemingly more conventional in their use of pronouns. Touchstone mostly uses 'thou' to Audrey, whilst she uses 'you' to him. However, there is the possibility that Touchstone's use of 'thou' is as much one of belittlement as of love, with Touchstone viewing himself as the social superior.

The relationship between Rosalind and Orlando is a complex one, given that for most of the play Orlando believes Rosalind to be a boy called Ganymede, who sometimes pretends to be his beloved. When they first meet, Rosalind and Orlando address each other as 'you', as might be expected. When they meet again in the forest in 3.2, Rosalind continues to use this form.

Orlando varies in his use of pronouns. He twice uses 'prithee', and, when he is at his most emotional trying to convince Ganymede of his love for Rosalind, he moves from 'you' to 'thee': 'Fair youth, I would I could make thee believe I love' (370–1); 'I swear to thee, youth, by the white hand of Rosalind, I am that he, that unfortunate he' (378–9). In 4.1 Orlando again begins by using 'you', only to move to 'thou' in the throes of his pretend wooing – 'And wilt thou have me?' – a form with which he remains until the end of the scene, keeping up the charade, but also revealing his true feelings towards Rosalind – 'For these two hours, Rosalind, I will leave thee' (165–6); 'By two o'clock I will be with thee again' (168–9).

Rosalind slips into the 'thou' form in dialogue with Orlando at only two points in the play: in 4.1 when she engages in the mock marriage – 'But I do take thee, Orlando, for my husband' (128–9) – continuing with this pronoun through most of her description of how she, Rosalind, will behave in marriage, and slipping back into it for 'Alas, dear love, I cannot lack thee two hours' (167), perhaps betraying this as a genuinely felt expression, and again in 5.2 when she first sees Orlando after his encounter with the lion – 'O, my dear Orlando, how it grieves me to see thee wear thy heart in a scarf' (19–20) – another genuine exclamation of love. Even in the final lines of the play when she gives herself to Orlando, it is with the same formal 'you' that she uses to her father:

> ROSALIND [*To Duke Senior*]
> To you I give myself, for I am yours.
> [*To Orlando*] To you I give myself, for I am yours
>
> (5.4.114–15)

The developments and changes in the relationship between Rosalind and Celia can also, in part, be plotted through their use of personal pronouns to one another. In Shakespeare's plays, it is quite usual for women speaking in private to use 'you' to one another; but Rosalind and Celia are cousins, and their use of the 'thou' form through much of the play indicates their closeness. Equally their use of the 'you' form indicates a certain distance or reserve. We are going to look at two moments in the play that evidence this nuanced use of pronouns.

When we first encounter Rosalind and Celia in 1.2. Celia is attempting to persuade Rosalind into a better humour. She uses 'thou' to Rosalind, whilst Rosalind uses 'you' in return:

> CELIA
> I pray thee, Rosalind, sweet my coz, be merry.
> . . .
> ROSALIND
> Unless you could teach me how to forget a
> banished father you must not learn me how to
> remember any extraordinary pleasure.
>
> (1.2.1–7)

However, by line 40, when Rosalind and Celia are engaged in their playful mockery of Fortune, Rosalind moves to 'thou', perhaps an indication of her change of mood:

> ROSALIND
> Nay, now thou goest from Fortune's office to Nature's
>
> (1.2.40–1)

A similar use of pronouns can be found in 3.2 in Rosalind and Celia's dialogue following Celia's discovery of the identity of the author of the poems. Celia begins using 'thou' as she attempts to draw Rosalind in: 'Dids't thou hear these verses?' (160). Rosalind responds with 'you'. Suddenly Celia, deciding that she is going to have some fun with her knowledge by concealing it from Rosalind, moves to 'you': 'Trow you who hath done this?' (174), and Rosalind, desperate to know what Celia has discovered, moves to 'thou': 'I prithee, who?' (178). These two moments indicate the way in which readers and performers, if they pay close attention to the characters' use of personal pronouns, can infer moments of closeness and distance, of intimacy and reserve.

Asides and soliloquies

The introduction discussed the conventions of asides and soliloquies within the context of the Elizabethan theatre. It also explored the disagreements that have arisen over what might constitute an aside or soliloquy, partly as a result of the rarity of the term 'aside' in the early printed texts of Shakespeare's plays. *As You Like It* is quite rare in the Shakespearean canon, in that it contains only one soliloquy (not including the epilogue spoken by the actor playing Rosalind): one moment when a character, on stage alone, speaks their thoughts aloud. This moment comes in the first scene of the play when Oliver, following the departure of Charles the Wrestler, reveals his true feelings and intentions:

> OLIVER Now will I stir this
> gamester. I hope I shall see an end of him; for my soul
> – yet I know not why – hates nothing more than he. Yet
> he's gentle, never schooled and yet learned, full of noble
> device, of all sorts of enchantingly beloved, and indeed so
> much in the heart of the world, and especially of my
> own people, who best know him, that I am altogether
> misprized. But it shall not be so long. This wrestler
> shall clear all. Nothing remains but that I kindle the boy
> thither, which now I'll go about.
>
> (1.1.153–62)

The speech could be delivered as a self-address, but we should at least be open to the possibility of it being addressed to the audience, and ask ourselves what it might mean for an audience to be directly addressed by a character.

In spite of editorial disagreements, there are a few moments that feel indisputably like self-addresses or addresses to the audience, in that they are not delivered to anyone on stage – Orlando's 'I am more proud to be Sir Rowland's son . . . Frederick' (1.2.221–3); 'Can I not say I thank you . . .' (1.2.238–40); Rosalind's 'I could find it in my heart to disgrace my man's apparel . . .' (2.4.4–8); Touchstone's musings on marriage in 3.3: 'I am not in the mind . . .' (3.3.82–5) and Oliver Martext's 'Tis no matter . . .' (3.3.98–100). As was discussed in Chapter 1, the main speaker of obvious asides in *As You Like It* is Jaques, in keeping with his status as a wry commentator (3.3.8–9, 29, 42). By contrast, Rosalind's asides are mostly to Celia, indicative of Celia's status as her confidante:

> ROSALIND
> I will speak to him like a saucy lackey and
> under that habit play the knave with him. – Do you
> hear, forester?
>
> (3.2.287–9)

The actor will decide the most appropriate mode of delivery depending on the style of production and conception of the character, and, of course, in many Shakespeare productions actors choose to play additional lines as asides, irrespective of whether or not they are marked as such by editors.

Rhetoric

The introduction explored the influence of Shakespeare's education and reading on his understanding and use of rhetoric. *As You Like It* abounds with rhetorical devices, placed in the mouths of a number of different characters. Brian Vickers refers to the 'matching brilliance of Touchstone and Rosalind' as users of rhetoric (1971: 94). He might also have included Jaques in this statement, since, as we will see, Jaques is also a master of language.

Touchstone is certainly the character who most obviously, and indeed self-consciously, employs the rhetorical methods of *elocutio, inventio, dispositio, memoria* and *pronuntiatio*, the five key areas of rhetorical training explored in the introduction (style, development of the argument, organization of the argument, memorization of the argument, delivery of the argument).

Indeed, Jaques comments on Touchstone's use of rhetoric in 2.7 when he says that 'he hath strange places crammed / With observation, the which he vents / In mangled forms' (40–2), 'places' being short for commonplaces or stock topics of rhetoric which Touchstone mangles, either inadvertently or deliberately, in his role as professional fool. A commonplace was a common topic, or commonly used line of argument, from which a rhetorical debate could be constructed. Amongst the commonplace topics listed by Aristotle in Book II of his *Rhetoric*, are 'ambiguous terms', 'meaning of names', and 'time' (D'Angelo, 1984: 58) the topic on which Jaques quotes Touchstone – 'And so from hour to hour we ripe and ripe, / And then from hour to hour we rot and rot' (2.7.26–7). Neil Rhodes suggests that it is a 'spirit of rivalry with the fool' that leads Jaques, having heard Touchstone's speech, to deliver 'the most famous commonplace set speech in Shakespeare' – 'All the World's a Stage' (2.7.140–67) (2004: 161), another meditation on time and the process of ageing.

As noted in the introduction, Shakespeare would have learnt about rhetoric as part of his grammar-school education; an education based on the work of Erasmus. Alison Thorne identifies the influence of Erasmus's textbook, *De duplici copia verborum ac rerum,* on *As You Like It*. Erasmus advocated the use of 'abundant style' and the ability to 'turn one idea into more shapes than Proteus himself' (quoted in Thorne, 2000: 9). Thorne suggests that it is in the pursuit of these ideas that Duke Senior and his fellow exiles 'find their chief recreation':

> Seeking to exploit the rich discursive possibilities presented by their experience of love and country living, they constantly rework these themes by visiting all the sources of eloquence mapped in *De Copia* (a process parodied by Touchstone's comic display of varying at V.1.45–57).

(2000: 10)

Duke Senior's first speech (2.1.1–17) is a perfect example of this. His proposition (*protasis*) is that their life in the forest is 'more sweet' than that at the court (2.1.2). He develops this idea over seventeen lines, offering a series of examples: 'Are not these woods / More free from peril than the envious court?' (2.1.3–4) to come to his final conclusion (*sumperasma*): 'And this our life, exempt from public haunt, / Finds tongues n trees, books in the running brooks, / Sermons in stones and good in everything' (2.1.15–17). The 'parody' in which Touchstone engages comes in his altercation with William (5.1.45–57), his proposal being that William 'perishest' (51), a *protasis* that he develops by offering a series of synonyms for killing: 'Or to thy better understanding, diest. Or (to wit) I kill thee, make thee away, translate thy life into death, thy liberty into bondage' (51–4), followed by a range of methods by which such a murder might happen:

> I will deal in poison with thee, or in bastinado
> or in steel. I will bandy with thee in faction; I will
> o'errun thee with policy. I will kill thee a hundred and
> fifty ways!
>
> (5.1.54–7)

The conclusion is brief: 'Therefore tremble and depart' (57).

Moments earlier in the scene Touchstone draws attention to his use of rhetorical tropes and figures: 'For it is a figure in rhetoric that drink, being poured out of a cup into a glass, by filling the one doth empty the other' (41–3). It is uncertain as to which figure he refers to, but Touchstone is clearly attempting to confuse and belittle William with what Keir Elam describes as his 'cultural one-upmanship' (1984: 241). Dusinberre cites the 'figure' as 'amplification', which even if it does not aptly describe the image of the drink, describes perfectly Touchstone's attack on William cited above, amplification being, according to Burke, the process of 'saying something in various ways until it increases in persuasiveness by the sheer accumulation' (1950: 69). Touchstone also makes use of the figure of *anaphora* (the repetition of the same words or words at the beginning of successive clauses) throughout his speech in the repetition of 'which in', 'or' and 'I will' at the start of clauses.

Figures of repetition abound in the speeches of a number of different characters, particularly in the final scenes of the play, which become increasingly artificial leading up to the highly patterned wedding ceremony. Rosalind, like Touchstone, draws attention to her use of rhetoric in her description of the meeting of Celia and Oliver:

For your brother and my sister no sooner
met but they looked; no sooner looked but they
loved; no sooner loved but they sighed; no sooner
sighed but they asked one another the reason; no
sooner knew the reason but they sought the remedy;
and in these degrees have they made a pair of stairs
to marriage, which they will climb incontinent, or
else be incontinent before marriage:

(5.2.31–8)

This speech is replete with the devices of *alliteration* (the repetition of consonant sounds – looked ... loved; sooner ... sighed); *anaphora* (the repetition of a word or words at the beginning of successive clauses) and *isocolon* (the repetition of phrases or clauses of equal length) in the repeated 'no sooner ...' phrases; *anadiplosis* (the repetition of the last word of one clause at the start of another) and *gradatio* (the pattern of repeating the last word of a clause at the beginning of the next over a series of building instances) in the pattern 'no sooner met ... looked; no sooner looked ... loved; no sooner loved ... sighed; no sooner sighed'. *Gradatio* was otherwise known by the Greeks as 'the staircase', progressing as it does, step by step to its climax. Thus, when Rosalind states that 'in these degrees have they made a pair of stairs to marriage', she is deliberately punning on the very nature of the rhetorical device that she is using.

This, of course, brings us to the highly patterned dialogue (5.2.80–101) which comes later in this same scene. This dialogue, beginning with Silvius's 'It is to be all made of sighs and tears' (80) makes extensive use of *anaphora*, in the repeated 'And' and 'All' at the start of phrases, and *isocolon*, in the repeated phrases of equal length: 'And I for ...' and 'It is to be all made ...'. The effect is an elaborate parody in which all the Petrarchan lovers indulge before Rosalind cuts them off short: 'Pray you no more of this' (5.2.105).

The style of dialogue continues into the last scene of the play in which we get another series of highly patterned lines from a number of characters:

ROSALIND [*To Duke Senior*]
   To you I give myself, for I am yours.
   [*To Orlando*] To you I give myself, for I am yours.

DUKE SENIOR
　If there be truth in sight, you are my daughter.
ORLANDO
　If there be truth in sight, you are my Rosalind.
PHOEBE
　If sight and shape be true,
　Why then, my love adieu.
ROSALIND
　I'll have no father, if you be not he.
　I'll have no husband, if you be not he.
　Nor ne'er wed woman, if you be not she.

(5.4.114–22)

Once again, we see the use of *anaphora* (the repetition of the same word or words at the beginning of successive clauses), *isocolon* (the repetition of phrases or clauses of equal length) and *epistrophe* (phrases ending with the same words) and also *symploce* (the use of *anaphora* and *epistrophe* together (repetition of the first and last words of each line) as is found in lines 120–1). These figures provide a sense of heightened ceremony to the passage. Even Jaques indulges in this intensified rhetorical mode, maintaining a sense of ritual, but one that, as might be expected, he deliberately undermines with the sting in the tail of his final 'blessing' to Touchstone and Audrey:

[*To Duke Senior*] You to your former honour I bequeath;
Your patience and your virtue well deserves it.
[*to Orlando*] You to a love that your true faith doth merit;
[*to Oliver*] You to your land and love and great allies:
[*to Silvius*] You to a long and well-deserved bed;
[*to Touchstone*] And you to wrangling, for thy loving
　　voyage
Is but for two months victualled.

(5.4.184–9)

The scenes in the forest then finish on a series of rhyming couplets, maintaining a sense of ritual until the scene's end.
　Rosalind's prose epilogue might seem to introduce a note of informality; a relaxed conversational tone after the ritualistic patterning of the final act. However, this speech is also highly

rhetorical in its structure, being mostly constructed around the figure of *antithesis*: 'lady ... epilogue', 'lord ... prologue'; 'good wine ... no bush', 'good play ... no epilogue'; 'good bushes ... good plays', 'neither a good epilogue ... nor ... good play'; 'Oh women ... love you bear to men', 'O men .. love you bear to women' (Epilogue, 1–14). There is also notable use of *isocolon* (repetition of phrases of equal length) in the phrases 'I charge you, O women for the love you bear to men' and 'I charge you, O men, for the love you bear to women' (Epilogue, 11–14) and *isocolon* and *syncrisis* (the figure of comparison and contrast in parallel clauses) in the lines 'If is be true that good wine needs no bush, 'tis true that a good play needs no epilogue' (3–4). The clauses are of similar structure and equal length and present parallel comparisons. It seems fitting that a play so concerned with rhetoric should be furnished with a final speech that displays such balance and patterning, and that it should be put in the mouth of one of its most eloquent characters.

Writing matters

Prose to verse

In this chapter we looked at the abrupt move from prose to verse in 1.3.
 There is a similar move in 1.2, at around line 213:

> DUKE FREDERICK
> I would thou hadst been son to some man else.
>
> (1.2.213)

Look at this moment in 1.2 and consider how and why the scene might move from prose to verse at this point, and stay in verse for the remainder of the scene. You might consider the characters and the situation.

The function of prose

In looking at the move from verse to prose in 1.3 (line 38), we considered the different views of Margery Garber, Peter Hall and Giles Block about the function of prose: Garber's suggestion that a shift from prose to verse indicates a 'change from intimacy to formality', the suggestion made by Hall that prose has a deliberate heightened 'formality' and the assertion made by Block that prose is medium of concealment whilst verse indicates an expression of true feelings. I briefly considered the impact that these different readings might have on the portrayal of Rosalind in this scene, offering two playable alternatives. Consider the arguments of Hall, Block and Garber, and use them to make a case for the playing of this scene in a particular way. Consider the impact on all three characters.

Orlando's verses

In this chapter we looked at different metres used in the play, most notably for the poems composed by Orlando, which are in tetrameter.

> ROS. *From the east to westerne Inde,*
> *no iewel is like Rosalinde,*
> *Hir worth being mounted on the winde,*
> *through all the world beares Rosalinde.*
> *All the pictures fairest Linde,*
> *are but blacke to Rosalinde:*
> *Let no face bee kept in mind,*
> *but the faire of Rosalinde.*
>
> (F1, TLN.1286–1293)

I mentioned that the parallel poem about Rosalynde in Lodge's novel is also in tetrameter. Compare Orlando's poem with the poem in Lodge's *Rosalynde*, looking at metre, use of language, rhyme etc. Note – in Elizabethan English *v* is written as *u* in the middle of a word.

> ROSALYNDES DESCRIPTION
> *Like to the cleere in hig[h]est spheare*   [*cleere* – brightness]
> *Where all imperiall glorie shines,*
> *Of selfe same colour is her haire*
> *Whether unfolded or in twines:*
> *Heigh ho, faire Rosalynde.*
> *Her eyes are Saphires set in snow,*
> *Refining heauen by euerie winke;*

The Gods doo feare when as they glow,
And I doo tremble when I thinke.
Heigh ho, would she were mine.
Her cheeks are like the blushing clowde
That beautifies Auroraes *face,* [Auroraes – belonging
Or like the silver crimson shrowde to the Roman
 goddess of the dawn]
That Phoebus *smiling looks doth grace:* [Phoebus – Roman
Heigh ho, faire Rosalynde. god of the sun]
Her lippes are like two budded roses,
Whoom rankes of lillies neighbour nie,
Within which bounds she balme incloses,
Apt to intice a Deitie: [*Deitie* – God]
Heigh ho, would she were mine.
Her necke like to a stately towre,
Where Loue himself imprisoned lies,
To watch for glaunces euerie howre,
From her deuine and sacred eyes,
Heigh ho, faire Rosalynde.
Her pappes are centers of delight, [*pappes* – breasts]
Here pappes are orbes of heauenlie frame,
Where Nature moldes the deaw of light,
To feede perfection with the same:
Heigh ho, would she were mine.
With orient pearle, with rubie red,
With marble white, with saphire blew,
Her bodie euerie way is fed;
Yet soft in touch, and sweete in view:
Heigh ho, faire Rosalynde.
Nature her selfe her shape admires,
The Gods are wounded in her sight,
And Loue forsakes his heauenly fires,
And at her eyes his brand doth light:
Heigh ho, would she were mine.
Then muse not Nymphes though I bemoane
The absence of faire Rosalynde:
Since for her faire is fairer none,
Nor for her vertues so deuine.
Heigh ho faire Rosalynde:

> *Heigh ho my heart, would God that she were mine.*
> (Lodge, 1590: H4v–I1v)

Rhyme

In this chapter we looked at the use of rhyme in *As You Like It*, considering its dramatic function.

> ORLANDO
>   And ere we have thy youthful wages spent
>   We'll light upon some settled low content.
> ADAM
>   Master, go on and I will follow thee
>   To the last gasp of truth and loyalty.
>   From seventeen years till now almost fourscore
>   Here lived I, but now live here no more.
>   At seventeen years many their fortunes seek,
>   But at fourscore it is too late a week.
>   Yet fortune cannot recompense me better
>   Than to die well and not my master's debtor.
> (2.3.67–76)

Personal pronouns

In the discussion about Shakespeare's use of personal pronouns ('you' and 'thou'), I looked at Rosalind and Celia's use of personal pronouns in lines 160–78 of 3.2. Look at the remainder of their dialogue in this scene (lines 179–243) and consider the significance of Rosalind and Celia's use of 'you' and 'thou' (and their attendant parts of speech).

Monosyllables

In the latter part of this chapter we explored monosyllabic lines, which, I suggested, are often used for emphasis or to reinforce pithy sayings, as well as by characters who might be tentative in their speech. See if you can find two monosyllabic lines not explored above and explain what you feel is the significance or dramatic effect of the use of monosyllables. You might want to look for two contrasting lines.

CHAPTER THREE

Language Over Time

This chapter considers some issues relating to the language of *As You Like It* that have arisen over the period since it was written. It begins by asking some provocative questions that emerge from gaps or contradictions in the text: 'How tall is Rosalind?', 'Who is called Frederick?', 'What is the clown's name?' It then moves on to look at moments in the play that may seem obscure to a modern audience due to developments in language over the past four hundred years, or as a result of the inclusion of direct contemporary references or allusions. Considering the changing meaning of words, and the presence of expressions that are now archaic or obsolete, it looks at the recent fashion for making changes to the text in performance in order to make the play more accessible to modern audiences. Finally, it considers key issues of interpretation on stage and screen and their impact on the language of the play, including recent trends in cross-gendered casting; the way in which the depiction of the court and forest on the stage can necessitate a change in scene order; and the way in which elements of language become redundant or problematic when the play is filmed for cinema or television.

Issues of interpretation

As was discussed in the introduction, the play of *As You Like It* was first published in 1623, in the Shakespeare First Folio (F1). This means that there is essentially only one substantive original text, as the re-prints of the Folio in 1632 (F2), 1664 (F3) and 1685 (F4) contain only minor emendations or alterations to F1. Dusinberre suggests that the 'elegant and unproblematic presentation in the Folio has perhaps allowed various mistakes in the text to go unchallenged' (2006: 125). Certainly over the years editors have questioned some of the speech attributions, seemingly odd word choices and small inconsistencies that are present in the text as presented in the Folio, and have made various suggestions for their emendation, as well as updating old spelling and making alterations to punctuation in accordance with modern grammar. Most of these emendations are minor; however, a few are worth discussing for their impact on theatrical delivery and characterization.

Is Rosalind merry or weary?

When Rosalind, Celia and Touchstone enter the Forest of Arden, in the Folio text Rosalind declares: 'O Jupiter, how merry are my spirits?' (2.4.1). Most editors emend 'merry' to 'weary', anticipating Touchstone's rejoinder 'I care not for my spirits, if my legs were not weary' (2.4.2–3) and Rosalind's subsequent comment that she could 'find in my heart to disgrace my man's apparel and to cry like a woman' (2.4.4–5). In doing so, they assume that the compositor responsible for printing this passage in the Folio mistook a secretary-hand *w* for an *m*, the two being quite similar. However, although 'weary' is accepted as a reading by most modern editors, there remain objections to this emendation from editors who believe that Rosalind's initial line is a case of deliberate affectation of merriness or deliberately ironic. One might argue that the impact on characterization is negligible, since Rosalind is clearly tired and close to tears; however, it surely says something about her character – and perhaps about her perception of her role as 'Ganymede' – if she shows to Celia only a positive outlook, whilst acknowledging to Touchstone (in what must then be played as an aside) her true feelings. Most productions of the play use Lewis Theobald's editorial emendation 'weary', with recent exceptions being Gregory Thompson's 2003 RSC production and Maria Aberg's 2013 RSC production.

How rude is Rosalind?

Another very minor point of variance, but one that may also be seen to have some impact on the perception of Rosalind's character, occurs at 1.2.104. The issue is over a single letter 'o'; whether Rosalind's line should read 'Thou loosest thy old smell' (as it does in F) or 'Thou losest thy old smell' as suggested by Rowe (1709), one of the earliest editors of Shakespeare's plays. If the latter is assumed, then Rosalind's response to Touchstone's 'Nay, if I keep not my rank' is merely wordplay on the word 'rank' (meaning both status and smell). If Touchstone doesn't keep his 'rank', he loses his 'smell'. However, if the Folio reading is retained Rosalind's response is potentially quite a lot ruder, referring to the letting loose of a smell, or breaking wind. Le Beau's line 'You amaze me, ladies' consequently may become less an exclamation of confusion at the banter that he doesn't understand, and more an exclamation of shock at Rosalind's unladylike humour. In the theatre, even when 'losest' is retained some Rosalinds make explicit the farting pun by including a rude noise or gesture. Michael Boyd, in his 2009 production of the play for the RSC, changed the line to 'thou let loose thy old smell', making the joke particularly clear.

Such punning is certainly not out of character for Rosalind, particularly once in the Forest of Arden. However, even before this, in 1.3, she makes a sexual pun which some editors and theatre producers, particularly in the eighteenth and nineteenth centuries, deemed inappropriate for the character. When Celia questions Rosalind's silence asking her, 'But is all this for your father' (1.3.10), in the Folio text Rosalind responds 'No, some of it is for my child's father' (1.3.11), i.e. Orlando, the man who she would like to father her child. Editors from Rowe (1714) through to R. Grant White in 1883 (with the exception of Theobald) assumed Rosalind's line to be a vulgar error for the far more delicate 'for my father's child', i.e. herself. On stage the line was regularly cut or emended to 'father's child' until 1898.

What's that Ducdame?

Occasionally in *As You Like It,* as in many of Shakespeare's plays as printed in the early modern texts, there is a question over the attribution of certain lines. Sometimes it appears that the author, scribe or compositor may have made an error in the transcription or printing of the text, providing the wrong speech prefix. In many cases these errors are uncontroversial and easy to emend. In 3.3, for example, the Folio gives the speech prefix Ol[iver] for the lines 'Come, sweet Audrey, / We must be married, or we must live in bawdry . . .' (88). These lines clearly belong to Touchstone and not to Sir Oliver Martext, and F2 emended the speech prefix to Clo[wn]. In other instances there remains some editorial and theatrical variation in the attribution of lines.

In 2.5 Jaques gives Amiens a verse of a song, which Amiens then offers to sing. In the Folio, the ensuing lines run as follows:

AMY.   And Ile sing it.

AMY.   Thus it goes.
If it do come to passe, that any man turne Asse:
Leauing his wealth and ease,
A stubborne will to please,
Ducdame, ducdame, ducdame:
Heere shall he see, grosse fooles as he,
And if he will come to me.

AMY.   What's that Ducdame?

(F1, TLN.935–943)

There is clearly some sort of error with the repeated speech prefixes for Amiens. The question is: what is the error? Was the compositor simply over-zealous in repeating a speech prefix when it was unnecessary; or, do we assume, as suggested by the printing of the lines in F2, that the second speech prefix should be for Jaques, who should also speak or sing the song; or, do we adopt editor C. J. S Sisson's emendation of 1954, which gives 'Thus it goes' to Jaques, with an accompanying stage direction, '[*Gives* AMIENS *a paper*]' and then assigns the song to Amiens; or indeed Dusinberre's emendation, which essentially follows Sisson, but assigns the final two lines of the song to All, making sense of the speech prefix for Amiens for 'What's that Ducdame?' (2006: 213). Editors continue to vary in their attribution of the words of the song. However, in the theatre they are most often assigned to Jaques, not least because they provide the opportunity for the actor to play up the aural pun of the first two lines. Whilst pass and ass would probably have rhymed in Elizabethan pronunciation with an æ phoneme (as in mat), in order to make them rhyme in English received pronunciation (the standard or neutral form of English pronunciation – based on 'educated speech in southern England' (OED)), 'ass' must be pronounced as 'arse'. To describe his fellow man as an arse seems very much in keeping with Jaques' persona and mood.

Who's the merrier?

Another debated case of line attribution occurs at the start of 1.2 where the Folio prints the first six lines thus:

> CEL.   I pray thee *Rosalind*, sweet my Coz, be merry.
>
> ROS.   Deere *Cellia*; I show more mirth then I am mi-
> stresse of, and would you yet were merrier: vnlesse you
> could teach me to forget a banished father, you must not
> learne mee how to remember any extraordinary plea-
> sure.
>
> (F1, TLN.171–176)

Most editors follow Nicholas Rowe (1714) in inserting 'I' into Rosalind's line: 'and would you yet I were merrier'. However, the Arden Third Edition follows a suggestion made by W.C. Jourdain (1860–1: 143) that the lines have been wrongly attributed, giving the words 'And would you yet were merrier' to Celia:

> CELIA
>   I pray thee, Rosalind, sweet my coz, be merry.
> ROSALIND
>   Dear Celia, I show more mirth than I am mistress of.
> CELIA
>   And would you yet were merrier.
> ROSALIND
>   Unless you could teach me to forget a banished father you
>   must not learn me how to remember any extraordinary
>   pleasure.
>
> (Dusinberre, 2006: 160).

The Rowe emendation has almost always been played on stage, probably because it is what most directors find in the edition that they consult. However, either emendation is equally playable.

Which Duke is called Frederick?

I now move to three more substantial issues of textual debate, the first of which also involves questions about line attribution. The passage in question is in 1.1 and reads as follows in the Folio:

> CEL. Prethee, who is't that thou means't?
> CLO. One that old *Fredericke* your Father loues.
> ROS. My Fathers loue is enough to honor him enough; speake no more of him, you'l be whipt for taxation one of these daies.
>
> (F1, TLN.246–50)

This passage suggests that the Clown's line is directed to Rosalind, and yet, Frederick appears to be the name of the usurping Duke, as indicated at 1.2.223 and again at 5.4.152:

> ORLANDO
> I am more proud to be Sir Rowland's son,
> His youngest son, and would not change that calling
> To be adopted heir to Frederick.
>
> (1.2.221–3)

> JAQUES DE BOYS
> Duke Frederick, hearing how that every day
> Men of great worth resorted to this forest,
>
> (5.4.152–3)

As H. H. Furness suggests 'one of two changes must be made. Either the name of Frederick must be changed, or the answer given to Rosalind in line 79, must be given to Celia' (1890: 28). Most editors follow the latter suggestion, reassigning the line; however Dusinberre follows Edward Capell's suggestion (1767–8), changing Frederick to Ferdinand (a name first assigned to the duke in the dramatis personae of the Douai manuscript – a collection of some of Shakespeare's plays transcribed in around 1694). The alteration to Ferdinand does make slightly better sense of the epithet 'old', which some productions, electing to keep the reference to Frederick, alter to 'Duke'. Dusinberre also suggests that if the reference is to Rosalind's father (as played in David Thacker's 1992 RSC production), then the 'certain knight' that he loves 'may be his own brother', and thus, Rosalind is jumping to Celia's defence as much as to her father's (2006: 165). Of course, the knight may still be Celia's father, even if the lines are assigned to Celia – as they were in Steven Pimlott's 1996 RSC production – the implication being that Celia's father loved himself (Tennant, 1998: 36).

How tall is Rosalind?

Another issue over which there is some question is the relative heights of Rosalind and Celia. In 1.3, when Rosalind and Celia make the decision to escape to Arden, Rosalind asserts:

> ROSALIND   Were it not better,
> Because that I am more than common tall,
> That I did suit me all points like a man?
>
> (1.3.111–13)

This line often becomes the impulse for casting a tall actress as Rosalind. The reference is supported by Oliver's lines in 4.3 where he reports the instructions that he has been given to find Ganymede and Aliena, namely:

> OLIVER   'The boy is fair,
> Of female favour, and bestows himself
> Like a ripe sister; the woman low,
> And browner than her brother'.
>
> (4.3.84–7)

However, in 1.2, when Orlando asks Monsieur Le Beau which of Rosalind and Celia is 'daughter of the duke / That here was at the wrestling?' he replies:

LE BEAU
   Neither his daughter, if we judge by manners,
   But yet indeed the taller is his daughter.
   The other is daughter to the banished Duke,

(1.2.261–3)

This implies that Celia is the taller of the two women. It is possible that the word 'taller' is simply an error here. However, it is also possible that the inconsistency reflects the practices of Shakespeare's company – that the original Celia either had a growth spurt – outgrowing the Rosalind, or that a new actor took on the role and that these lines needed to be changed accordingly. It is quite possible that such an emendation might make its way into a prompt book, and hence into the Folio text. Editors have variously emended the line to 'shorter', 'smaller', 'lower' or 'lesser' and productions have followed suit. In cases where a decision has been made to have a small Rosalind, and thus retain the reference to Celia's height, it is quite straightforward to cut the reference to her being 'more than common tall' to make Rosalind's lines in 1.3 read: 'Were it not better, / That I did suit me all points like a man?' (1.3.107–9). Very few productions, though, bother to make a corresponding emendation to the lines in 4.3.

What's the Clown's name?

Throughout the F1 text, the speech prefix for the character of 'Touchstone' is *Clo.* or '*Clow.*' and in stage directions he is referred to as '*Clowne*'. The only exception to this is the stage direction for the characters' entrance into Arden in 2.4.0, which reads '*Enter Rosaline for Ganimed, Celia for Aliena, and Clowne*, alias *Touchstone*'. The word 'alias' is defined by the OED as 'An alternative name for a person or thing; *esp.* a false or assumed name' (2020). This raises the possibility that 'Touchstone' is a name that the fool adopts when he enters the forest, just as Rosalind becomes 'Ganymede' and Celia, 'Aliena'. Prior to entering the forest, Rosalind and Celia only refer to him and address him as 'Fool'. It's not until they enter the forest that Rosalind first calls him 'Touchstone' (2.4.17), a name also used by Corin in 3.2 (ll.12 and 43). Lewis Theobald, in his second edition of 1740, regularized all speech prefixes and stage directions for '*Clowne*' to '*Touchstone*', and this practice has been followed by most editors since. However, H. H. Furness, in his Variorum edition of the play argued that Theobald may have committed a 'serious' 'error' in doing so. Furness's objection was not based on the issue of whether 'Touchstone' was, indeed, the Clown's given name, but on his conviction that the change in speech prefixes and stage directions was indicative of the presence of two separate characters – a Fool in Duke Frederick's court, and a second 'clown' figure, Touchstone, who accompanies Rosalind and Celia into the Forest of Arden. For Furness, this likelihood, indicated by the change in speech prefix, stage direction and terms of address was further evidenced by what he, and others, saw as a significant inconsistency in the character. Furness asks:

> Is the 'clownish fool' and the 'roynish clown' of the First Act, with his bald jests of knights and pancakes, the Touchstone of the fifth act, who has trod a measure, flattered a lady, been politic with his friend and smooth with his enemy? Is the simpleton of the First Act, 'Nature's natural', as he is in truth, the same with the Touchstone who can cite Ovid and quarrel in print, by the book? Are there not here two separate characters? These two clowns cannot be one and the same.
>
> (Furness, 1890: 309)

Furness's view does not seem to have received any traction, either in editorial practice, or in the theatre, where the role seems always to have been conceived as a single figure, most often referred to in dramatis personae by the name 'Touchstone'.

Contemporary references, changing meanings and archaic language

Like other of Shakespeare's plays, *As You Like It* contains a number of lines that may prove difficult for the modern reader, actor or audience member to decipher. Some contain contemporary allusions, which may have been immediately recognizable to readers, actors and theatre goers in 1599, but are no longer accessible to their contemporary counterparts. Others make reference to elements of Elizabethan theatre practice that are now obsolete, whilst many contain words that have either fallen out of the common vernacular, or whose meanings have changed since the sixteenth century. Whilst these elements can prove challenging to the modern reader, editions of the plays are able to provide detailed footnotes that help to gloss obscure words and references. In the theatre this is not possible. As a result there are some lines that are now rarely included in modern productions and others that are habitually changed in order to accommodate contemporary theatre practice, sensibilities and common knowledge.

Alas, poor shepherd

Although Shakespeare's plays contain frequent allusions to the time in which he lived and wrote, they contain relatively few direct contemporary references. Indeed, Gary Taylor argues that the reference to the anticipated return of the Earl of Essex in *Henry V* ('As, by a lower but loving likelihood, / Were now the general of our gracious empress, / As in good time he may, from Ireland coming'; 5.0.29–31) is 'the only explicit, extra-dramatic, incontestable reference to a contemporary event anywhere in the canon' (1982: 7). The return of the second Earl of Essex, Robert Devereux (who was one of the queen's favourites), to England following his military campaign in Ireland was much anticipated (although in the end he returned without permission and mounted a rebellion against the queen).

Nevertheless, *As You Like It* seemingly contains two references to the death of Christopher Marlowe, Shakespeare's contemporary, who died in 1593 in a tavern in Deptford supposedly in an argument over the bill. The most explicit of these is a line given to Phoebe, just after she has fallen in love with Rosalind as Ganymede:

> Dead shepherd, now I find thy saw of might:
> 'Whoever loved that loved not at first sight'
>
> (3.5.82–3)

The 'saw' quoted by Phoebe comes from Marlowe's narrative poem, *Hero and Leander,* written in 1593, but published posthumously in

1598 shortly before the composition of *As You Like It*. The poem was clearly popular; it was published in two editions in 1598, before a third in 1600, and one can assume that many of the more educated members of the audience would have recognized the quote, and understood the phrase 'Dead shepherd' to refer to Marlowe, who was famous for his pastoral verse as well as for his plays. The second apparent reference to Marlowe occurs in 3.3 where Touchstone states: 'When a man's verses cannot be understood ... it strikes a man more dead than a great reckoning in a little room' (3.3.10–13). Most recent editors have taken it to refer to Marlowe's death over a 'reckoning' or bill. In most productions of the play these lines are retained, perhaps because of the extensive academic discussion over the allusions, although their relevance, if not their gist, is probably lost on the majority of a contemporary audience. In an effort to make the first of these references more explicit, Michael Boyd in his 2009 RSC production changed 'Dead shepherd' to 'Dead poet'.

'To say ay and no to these particulars is more than to answer in a catechism'

In addition to passages which depend on a knowledge of the context in which the play was composed to be fully understood, there are other passages that are either particularly convoluted in their expression or replete with words that have dropped out of common usage. Since it is rare for any Shakespeare play to be performed in its entirety on the modern stage one finds these lines are regularly cut from theatre performances, such that some lines have seldom been spoken on the modern stage. One such example is Celia's line: 'To say ay and no to these particulars is more than to answer in a catechism' (3.2.219–21) which is almost invariably cut. This is doubtless because Celia's protestation relies on an audience having some knowledge of the catechism for children, printed in the *Book of Common Prayer*, which required children to give the answer yes ('ay') or no to a series of questions about Christianity, something with which few modern audience members are likely to be familiar.

Many of the lines that are commonly cut from modern performance are those containing classical allusions. Education in the late-twentieth and twenty-first centuries – unlike that which would have been received by the Elizabethan schoolboy – does not include classical Latin or Greek literature as a matter of course, and many audience members and theatre practitioners are thus less likely to be readily familiar with the mythological figures and events referred to in the texts than the play's original audiences.

Whilst words that have dropped out of common usage may pose a difficulty to a modern reader or audience, more challenging still are those words that have changed their meaning since the Renaissance. In 1.2, Le Beau comments of Duke Frederick, 'The Duke is humorous' (1.2.255). Far from meaning that the duke is amusing or funny, as one might expect from modern usage of the word, he means almost the opposite: that the duke is ill-tempered, volatile and irascible; subject to the four humours which were thought to create temperament in the Early Modern period. Such changes in meaning may prove confusing to the twenty-first-century ear or eye without further glossing or explanation.

Finally, there are lines within the play that no longer seem compatible with modern sensibilities about gender, race or religion. One such instance in *As You Like It* occurs in 4.3, where Rosalind exclaims of Phoebe's letter:

> **ROSALIND**
> Why, 'tis a boisterous and a cruel style,
> A style for challengers. Why, she defies me,
> Like Turk to Christian. Women's gentle brain
> Could not drop forth such giant-rude invention,
> Such Ethiop words, blacker in their effect
> Than in their countenance.
>
> (4.3.31–6)

This passage has been cut in the majority of modern productions of the play, presumably because of its racist overtones – both in its inference about the cruelty of the Turks, and in its use of 'Ethiop' as a negative metaphor. In fact the reference to the Turk and the Christian is less Shakespeare's own assessment of these two religious groups, and more obviously a reference to the confrontation between the Turkish knight and the Christian knight that occurred in the mumming plays performed at Christmas (early versions of pantomimes) that were intended to represent the struggle between good and evil. Sophie Chiari describes this 'topical reference to Christmas games' as 'part and parcel of a larger network of allusions' to winter in the play (2019: n. 80). However, this reference to an antiquated tradition is unlikely to be grasped by a modern audience.

The language of the Clown

The characters in Shakespeare who are often perceived as the most difficult for a modern reader or audience to understand are the clowns or fools, whose language is often full of puns that rely on complex wordplay and contemporary allusions. In an article in the *Telegraph* in 2015, both Richard Eyre, former artistic director of the National Theatre, and Ben Crystal were quoted as 'admit[ting]' that 'William Shakespeare's jokes are just not funny'. Eyre said, 'It's true that a lot of Shakespeare's jokes aren't very good . . . Because they're topical . . . Comedy dates very, very quickly', whilst Crystal explained, 'There are certainly plenty of jokes that simply don't make sense any more – these context-relevant jokes aren't funny because they're social commentary gags, and even with a broad understanding of Shakespeare's society, they're smirk-worthy at best' (Furness, 2015).

Touchstone's language is replete with such topical, rhetorically-complex puns, making some of his speeches difficult to comprehend without an in-depth understanding of social mores – duelling, beards, and the rules of rhetoric and public and private spheres. David Tennant, who played Touchstone at the RSC in 1996, admits that his first perception of the character was as 'stuffed with endless "routines" and thick with references which had lost any contemporaneousness about three hundred years ago' (1998: 30). Touchstone's speeches about the seven degrees of the lie in 5.4 have frequently been cut, sometimes altogether, as they were in Branagh's BBC version, the 2013 and 2019 RSC productions, and the National Theatre production of 2016.

However, contemporary actors have found ways of making Touchstone's humour work, sometimes with the addition of gesture or physical comedy, a particularly fast pace of delivery or a delivery that draws attention to the feat of memorization. As Lois Potter asserts, Touchstone's speeches in 5.4 are a 'clear case of an actor displaying his memory', something exploited by actor Roy Kinnear, who played the role at the RSC in 1967. According to Potter, 'in one performance, he either lost track, or pretended to lose track, of "the degrees of the lie", with the result that Jaques's line had the effect of a challenge from one actor to another and Kinnear's successful repetition of the list got audience applause' (1990: 92). Interestingly, Tennant, following his initial reservations about Touchstone's humour found that the best way to make the speeches work was not 'to smother the speech with comic business or vocal gymnastics' but to make it 'as intelligible as possible', treating the argument with increasing 'seriousness' (Tennant, 1998: 43). According to Robert Hanks, writing in the *Evening Standard*, Tennant's performance was 'one of the best pieces of Shakespearean clowning you're likely to see: actual Shakespeare jokes being actually funny' (Hanks, 1996).

Who killed the deer?

Another challenging section of *As You Like It* that is frequently cut in early productions of the play is 4.2, the scene containing the song 'Who killed the deer?', This is not so much for the difficulty in understanding its content as its purpose. While admitting that 'he couldn't work out how to do it', Nicholas Hytner, who cut the scene in its entirety in his 1986 production for the Manchester Royal Exchange, raises the point that for a modern audience the answer to the question 'Which is he that killed the deer?' is 'Who gives a fuck?' (Hytner, 2015). Indeed, it serves no particular narrative function, but it does provide a transition between two scenes involving Rosalind and Celia, between which a period of two hours is supposed to elapse. Hunting was a popular aristocratic sport in Elizabethan England, and Dusinberre suggests that 'some version of the song, which may have been a popular hunting round, was in existence at the time of Shakespeare's play' (2006: 133–4). However, it is perhaps more difficult to make the scene work for a modern audience, particularly given changes in attitudes towards hunting for pleasure.

In most nineteenth-century productions of the play, a stuffed deer was brought on stage and paraded around. Recent productions have experimented with other ways of conceiving and staging the scene. In Adrian Noble's 1985 RSC production the whole sequence was interpreted as Celia's dream:

> Jaques drew a bloodstained sheet across her as she slept, and the lords then pursued her around the stage as if she were the hunted deer. She had obviously had an erotic dream, a sexual awakening, and was therefore especially receptive to Oliver on his arrival, a point reinforced by the little laugh of sexual shock at his reference to the snake from which Orlando had saved him.
>
> (Warren, 1986: 116)

Gregory Thompson's production (RSC 2003) made a similar choice, with 'the body of the sleeping Celia' replacing that of the dead deer, thus anticipating 'the successful hunting by Oliver in the ensuing scene' (Dusinberre, 2006: 135). Polly Findlay's National Theatre production (2016) cut the scene completely, as did Maria Aberg (RSC 2013) who instead inserted a song for the four women – Rosalind, Celia, Phoebe and Audrey – to cover the transition in time.

Another difficulty with this scene is that it appears to produce an inconsistency in the character of Jaques, who in 2.1 is described by Amiens as weeping for the death of a deer wounded by a hunter, and yet in this scene appears to celebrate the killing. However, some have noted that the 'prize' that Jaques proposes for the victorious hunter – the wearing of horns on his head – is actually one that resembles the shaming devices used as part of a skimmington, a parade in which a cuckolded or hen-pecked husband was ridiculed. Kim Sykes' 2019 RSC production used this allusion to present the whole scene as a 'skimmington' in which Jaques 'punishes the forester for killing her deer' (Emma Baggott, interview). At the start of the scene, Sophie Stanton's Jaques set the horns on the head of the forester who had killed the deer, in apparent celebration and then tied his hands together. As the music began to play the forester capered, seemingly enjoying the celebration. But then Jaques began to jerk the rope and pull the forester to the ground, finally taking him up by the horns, and pulling his head back as she sang 'Is not a thing to laugh to scorn'. As well as making Jaques' attitude to hunting more consistent in its obvious condemnation of the forester, the reaction also seemed more in keeping with twenty-first-century attitudes towards the killing of animals for pleasure.

To modernize or not to modernize?

Writing in 2003, director Peter Hall asserted that 'In another 200 or so years, Shakespeare will only be faintly visible – rather as Chaucer is to us. Language must change or die. And Shakespeare's language will not always be comprehensible; he will soon need translating' (2003: 10). The perceived need to 'translate' Shakespeare has come sooner than Hall envisioned. The *No Fear Shakespeare* and *Shakespeare Made Easy* editions, which provide readers with a fully translated version of the plays, have become increasingly popular for use in classrooms and even rehearsal rooms, although the translated text is often incapable of conveying the nuances and double meanings in the Shakespearean original. In 2015, when the Oregon Shakespeare Festival announced their three year 'Play on Shakespeare' project – commissioning modern playwrights to 'translate all of Shakespeare's plays into modern English' (Shapiro, 2015) – there were a number of highly critical responses, followed by fierce debate. James Shapiro, writing in the *New York Times*, described the project as setting 'a disturbing precedent', arguing that 'the only thing Shakespearean about his plays *is* the language' (2015).

Oregon's project is an extreme example, and most mainstream theatres continue to work from scripts grounded firmly in the Shakespearean text; however, over recent years, directors have become increasingly prone to changing words that they feel a modern audience may not understand. Nicholas Hytner admitted to becoming gradually more comfortable with the idea of changing words if he felt that they might mislead an audience during his time at the National Theatre, changing, for example, the word 'doubt' to 'fear' in Hamlet's line 'My father's spirit in arms! I doubt some foul play' (1.2.256) and 'lets' to 'bars' in 'I'll make a ghost of him that lets me' (1.4.85) on the basis that both words now mean almost exactly the opposite of what they meant in Elizabethan England (Rokison-Woodall, 2017: 147).

In the case of *As You Like It,* recent productions at major British theatres have seen a marked increase in the number of word changes – with over twenty individual changes in the RSC 2019 production and over fifty in the National Theatre 2016 production. Some of the changes, in line with Hytner's *Hamlet* alterations, are to words meanings of which have changed, such that they might prove misleading to a modern ear. Orlando's description of Rosalind as 'unexpressive' (3.2.10) was altered to 'unexpressible' in Boyd's RSC production (2009) and to 'inexpressible' in Sykes' (2019), both of which words better convey a sense that Rosalind's qualities cannot be accurately described, whereas the original term might seem to suggest to the modern ear that she lacks expression. Similarly Audrey's assertion that William has 'no interest in me' (5.1.8) was changed in 2019 to 'no claim on me', since the former seems to convey the opposite of the truth about William's affections.

Other changes are to words that have dropped out of the modern vernacular – 'perforce' (1.2.20) becomes 'by force' (2016 NT and 2019 RSC), 'quintain' (1.2.240) becomes 'puppet' (2016 NT and 2019 RSC), 'battler' (2.4.46) becomes 'washboard' (2016 NT) or 'butter paddle' (RSC 2009 and 2016 NT), 'cods' (2.4.49) become 'peas' (2016 NT and 2019 RSC) and 'cote' (3.2.409), 'cottage' (2016 NT and 2019 RSC). These changes are broadly justified on the basis that productions want to be inclusive, ensuring that they make sense to everyone and that all audience members can access key information and jokes. Emma Baggott, assistant director on the RSC 2019 production, exemplifies this when she asserts that the alteration of 'tapster' to 'barman' (3.4.28) in Sykes' production reignited the humour in Celia's line – 'it gets a huge laugh, and why would you not allow an audience that response?' (Baggott, interview). In most cases the changes made do not affect the metre and simply serve to clarify, and it might seem churlish to raise objections about such minor points. However, questions remain as to the basis on which such decisions are made, the number of such alterations and where one draws the line. If a theatre director were to modernize every word that might need glossing to the average modern audience member, then we would soon be in the territory of almost wholesale 'translation'. However, as David Crystal points out, if they were only to translate words that have entirely dropped out of modern usage, then the case can only be made for around 5 per cent of Shakespeare's language (2002: 16). It is also the case that provided an actor knows what they are saying and why, meaning can usually be conveyed to an audience member who does not recognize the precise word or phrase. As actor Samuel West once pointed out, you don't need to know what 'fillip me with a three-man beetle' (*2H4*, 1.2.227) means to know that it is something fairly unpleasant that Falstaff would prefer to avoid (Rokison, 2005: 198).

Interpretation of language on the modern stage

Whilst many of the changes cited above are made on the basis of a perceived need to modernize language that might not be understood by a contemporary audience member, other changes and cuts to the text of *As You Like It* on the modern stage have been motivated by specific production choices, most notably the casting, setting and production design.

The Epilogue without the boy player

Although on the Early Modern stage the role of Rosalind would have been played by a boy player, in the majority of productions since the middle of the eighteenth century the part has been played by a woman. For most of the play, as with other female roles, no specific changes are required to the text in order to accommodate this theatrical convention. However, *As You Like It* is unusual in containing a direct reference to the boy player in the play's epilogue, in the words 'If I were a woman' (Epilogue, 16–18). Although Smallwood observed that, other than on two occasions (in 1973 when these words were cut and in 1992 when they were altered to 'As I am a woman'), on the RSC stage the epilogue had been 'given in full and unchanged' (2003: 212), in recent years there has been a greater tendency to tinker with the speech in order to reflect the presence of a woman in the role. In 2009 at the RSC, the speech was replaced by a variation on the traditional Scottish/Irish drinking song 'The Parting Glass' and in 2019 it was substantially re-written, both to make sense of it being spoken by a female actor and also to conform to the sensibilities of the production which was intended to be entirely inclusive of a range of gender identities and sexualities, thus removing all references to members of the audience as either 'women' or 'men':

> ROSALIND
> It is not the fashion to see the lady the Epilogue, but it is no more unhandsome than to see the lord the Prologue. It is true that a good play needs no epilogue. But good plays prove the better by the help of good epilogues. What a case am I in then,

that am neither a good epilogue, nor cannot insinuate with you in the behalf of a good play.

I am not furnished like a beggar, therefore to beg will not become me.

My way is to conjure you. I charge you all, to like as much of this play as please you. I could kiss as many of you as had complexions that liked me and breaths that I defied not. And I am sure as many as have good faces, or sweet breaths will for my kind offer, when I make curtsy, bid me farewell.

This sense of gender inclusivity extended further in the production, to the removal of derogatory gendered references – particularly to women. In Touchstone's line 'It is the first time that ever I heard breaking of ribs was sport for ladies' (1.2.130–2), the last two words were removed, as was Rosalind's reference to women as 'the weaker vessel' (2.4.6) at the start of 2.4. As will be seen, it also resulted in the 'ungendering' of one of the most famous speeches in the Shakespearean canon.

Cross-gender or gender-fluid casting on the modern stage

Whilst it has become increasingly common for the role of Rosalind to be played by a woman, it has, conversely, also become increasingly common for some of the roles originally conceived as male in Shakespeare's plays to be played by women. In 2015 ERA (Equal Representation for Actresses) was established with the aims of drawing attention to the gender imbalance on British stages and calling for 50:50 gender representation by 2020. In 2017 the new artistic director of Shakespeare's Globe, Michelle Terry, announced that there would be a 50–50 gender split on stage during her tenure; the National Theatre announced that by March 2021, 'as an average, there will be 50:50 gender balance on stage', and in 2019 the RSC announced that they had 'introduced a 50/50 gender balanced ensemble across the entire season for the very first time', a season that included Sykes' production of *As You Like It*.

The term 'cross-gender' in relation to casting is not a simple one. In the first place, it implies a binary distinction between genders, and whilst we can say with some certainty that Shakespeare created characters that are either male or female, unless we can be sure about the gender identity of the actor playing a role, the term can be problematic. Many critics now prefer the term 'gender fluid' with regards to casting practices. There is also a myriad of ways in which women can play roles that were originally written as male. A role can be played as gender neutral or gender fluid. A woman can play a male role as a man. In the latter case some prefer to use the term 'gender-blind casting' which infers that the audience is not supposed to see or notice the gender of the actor behind the character. However, as was discussed in relation to Early Modern audiences and boy players, one is forced to question whether audiences can ever be truly blind to the gender of an actor.

This is the form of casting that has been employed under Michelle Terry's artistic directorship at Shakespeare's Globe, and was referred to by one reviewer as 'post-gender' (Tripney, 2018) – grounded in a sense that a character's humanity is more significant than whether they are male or female. In the 2019 Globe production of *As You Like It*, Charles the Wrestler, Duke Frederick, Duke Senior, Orlando, Jaques, Amiens and Le Beau were all played by women, whilst Audrey and Rosalind were played by men. More common in the contemporary theatre is to change the gender of the character, so that a male character becomes female, as was the case in the RSC's 2019 production where Jaques and Amiens became female, Monsieur Le Beau became Madame, Silvius became Silvia and Sir Oliver Martext became Madame Olivia. This form of cross-gender casting necessitates changes to the language of the play in modes of address and personal pronouns. In Sykes' RSC production it had a more profound impact, most notably on Jaques' famous 'Seven Ages of Man' speech in 2.7, which, spoken by a female character, became 'Seven Ages of Person', resulting in a number of changes to the text rendering all the figures described gender neutral.

The order of scenes

The structure of *As You Like It* can prove challenging for a modern director. For many, the move from the 'perilous' court to the Forest of Arden seems to necessitate some sort of elaborate set piece or transformation in the setting. The problem with this is that unlike in *A Midsummer Night's Dream*, where once the characters are in the forest we remain there for three acts, in *As You Like It,* the setting moves back and forth between the court and the forest up until the end of 3.1.

This would, of course, have been unproblematic in a theatre like the Globe, where little scenery would have been employed and where the language dictated the setting as much as any visual cues. However, with the advent of more intricate theatrical design, directors 'routinely altered the order of the scenes in the first three acts . . . in the interests of not disturbing the scenery for the Forest of Arden' (Dusinberre, 2006: 137). In proscenium arch theatres there is usually the possibility of bringing in a curtain, in front of which can be played the two short scenes in Duke Frederick's court – 2.2 and 3.1; however, many productions, in a range of different spaces, choose to move or cut scenes in order to preserve the continuity of Arden. Dusinberre provides the example of Thompson's 2003 RSC production 'moving 2.2 back into Act 1', suggesting other alternatives as 'cutting 2.2 and 3.1, or replacing the earlier scene with the later one' (2006: 137). Thacker (1992 RSC) and Doran (2000 RSC) moved 2.2 and 2.3 to after 1.3, whilst Sykes (RSC 2019) and Findlay (NT 2016) played the scenes in the order 1.3–2.3–2.2, Sykes also moved 3.1 to immediately after this sequence, before moving into the forest. For Sykes, the move to Arden not only represented a change of locale, but also a stylistic transformation – a movement from a type of theatre defined by Peter Brook as 'Deadly' to one conceived as 'Rough' or 'Holy', a space in which the workings of the theatre were exposed and where the relationship between actor and audience became central. Once achieved, this movement into a new form could not reasonably be reversed.

Findlay's NT production made numerous other changes to the order of scenes, much as is often done in film or television, where long scenes are divided to avoid tedium – 3.5 was cut into three sections and a new scene for William and Audrey was written and introduced after 2.5. The effect was to distribute the minor characters more evenly across the Arden scenes, as though we, the audience, were located in a particular area of the forest through which the various characters passed at intervals. In an interview in the *Guardian*, Findlay described the 'episodic' plot of the play (which was even more episodic in her production) as 'the first sketch show ... Shakespeare ... trying to write the 1599 version of *The Fast Show*' (Dickson, 2015).

As You Like It on film: where pictures do the work

A medium in which it is easy to move back and forth between locations is that of film, and both Christine Edzard's (1992) and Kenneth Branagh's (2006) films rearrange and interlace scenes, moving seamlessly between the court and the forest. However, film presents its own challenges for presenting Shakespeare's plays. Cinema is as much a visual medium as an aural one, and is frequently concerned with showing as opposed to telling; quite different from the Early Modern theatre, in which, as has been discussed, the words often do the work in creating setting. As a result some of the more extended passages of speech in Shakespeare can feel at odds with the cinematic medium in which dialogue is often kept to a minimum.

Film is also generally conceived as a more 'realistic' genre than theatre, contained within a space the internal fiction of which is rarely broken. This has an effect on the translation of Shakespeare to the medium of modern cinema in terms of casting (the commonly accepted theatrical conventions of gender and colour-blind casting are yet to impact on the genre), setting, and the relationship between character and audience. The soliloquy, commonly presented in the theatre as conversation between a character and the audience, can be difficult to convey on film. Breaking the fourth wall is not a common filmic convention and neither is talking to oneself. Some film adaptations of Shakespeare employ the use of voice-over (more commonly used in film) to transform a soliloquy into a moment of silent contemplation in which we overhear a character's inner thoughts, but this can render speeches with an active intention passive. As a result some directors choose to cut soliloquies entirely, or to shorten them.

One of the key conventions of film is the ability to convey meaning without words, often through the use of montage. Thus, films can, and often do, provide backstory and exposition in the form of non-verbal sequences. In Shakespeare films such sequences can provide clarification, explanation and enhanced character motivation, and can obviate the need for expository and explanatory passages of dialogue. Branagh's film of *As You Like It,* for example, begins with a largely silent dramatization of the usurpation of Duke Senior by his brother. This provides the backstory to the play and removes the need for much of the conversation between Oliver and Charles the Wrestler in 1.1. We do not need to hear the lines about the lords who have 'put themselves into voluntary exile' (1.1.97) with Duke Senior since we see them in the montage of the duke entering the forest accompanied by various followers from the court.

Later in the film we are shown a dramatic sequence of Orlando saving Oliver from the lioness, meaning that the whole description of this moment can be cut from 4.3. Notable in both Edzard and Branagh's films is the absence of lines of dialogue that indicate the arrival of another character: 'Yonder sure they are coming' (1.2.140); 'Look, here comes the Duke' (1.3.36); 'Look you, who comes here?' (2.4.17–18); 'Here comes young master Ganymede' (3.2.83); 'Peace, here comes my sister reading' (3.2.120); 'Who comes here' (3.4.42), all of which are cut in both films. Such lines may serve the purpose on stage of covering the entrance of an actor or indicating the imminent arrival of an off-stage character, but neither is necessary on film where the character's arrival can be shown at any point in the dialogue.

With the addition of visual sequences and the expectation of 'the "ideal" running time of less than two hours' most films of Shakespeare plays use 'no more than 25–30 per cent of the original text' (Jackson, 2000: 17). Bearing this figure in mind, both Edzard and Branagh's films contain quite a high proportion of the original text, with Edzard retaining around 73 per cent and Branagh just over 50 per cent. Edzard's cut is striking in that it retains many of the more difficult passages of wordplay often removed in contemporary stage performances. Branagh's screenplay removes a lot more of this rhetorical, pun-ridden dialogue, leaving the bare bones of scenes. What Branagh's film does include, perhaps surprisingly, is Rosalind's epilogue. The epilogue seems a distinctively theatrical convention – a direct address to the audience by a figure in the liminal space between character and actor. Branagh finds a moment equivalent to the curtain call of a stage production – the film's closing credits. Bryce Dallas Howard steps out of the Arden set to where the location catering and trailers are parked, removing her jacket and handing it to a member of the crew, and thus she clearly transforms from Rosalind to the actress portraying the role. The transformation is fairly seamless, but the words of the epilogue feel rather awkward in this setting – the unchanged phrase 'like as much of this play as please you' jars in the filmic context, and the idea that the actor might be able to hear the men in the audience 'simpering' doesn't quite work. The moment has obvious parallels with Branagh's treatment of another speech that contains direct references to the theatre – the first Chorus to *Henry V* – which in Branagh's film of that play is spoken by Derek Jacobi as he moves through a cluttered sound stage exposing the workings of the film.

Writing matters

Textual matters

Imagine that you are directing a production of *As You Like It*. Choose one of the disputed textual examples given above and make an argument for why you would choose a particular reading.

Modernizing Shakespeare

David Crystal points out that although many words that Shakespeare uses are 'difficult', few have actually dropped out of common usage and many are so close to modern words that they are unlikely to cause concern (Crystal, 2002: 15–16). He concludes that 'over 90 per cent of the English used in Shakespeare's day has not lost its meaning', that it is not essential for an audience member – or even an actor – to know the precise meaning of a word in order to give it sense and that 'disassociating authors from the language they have carefully chosen to use hits deeply at their identity'. On this basis, he asserts that 'translation should only be employed after all other means of achieving comprehension have been explored' (Crystal, 2002: 17). Do you agree with Crystal or would you argue for the modernization of particular words and phrases? Justify your argument either way.

Gender-fluid casting

Can gender-fluid casting make us see characters in a new or different light? Provide examples for your answer.

CHAPTER FOUR

Performing the Language

Having explored the language of *As You Like It*, this final chapter thinks about how this language is performed by actors. It explores ideas about performing Shakespeare's verse, rhetoric and other forms of language on stage. It looks at modern attitudes to verse speaking and considers some of the main areas of debate and their impact on meaning. It also examines the way in which elements of rhetoric impact on the delivery of the lines and suggests exercises for practical exploration of elements including assonance, alliteration and antithesis. Finally, it considers ways of exploring the shifts in personal pronouns within the plays in order to explore character relationships.

Performing metre

When it comes to performing Shakespeare's verse there is some debate over how it should be spoken. Some of the key questions that emerge are:

- Should one make it naturalistic or formalistic?
- Should one make it prosaic or rhythmical?
- Should you speak it fast or slowly?
- Should you pause in the middle of a verse line or only ever at its end?

Academics continue to disagree about how Elizabethan actors would have spoken verse. In any case, most modern actors do not want to replicate the delivery of their forebears. However, a number of experienced and respected theatre practitioners writing in the past thirty years have disagreed with one another over the extent to which actors should be guided by the structure of the verse or by the grammatical structure of a passage; whether their delivery should have a formal quality, informed by the iambic pentameter (and its variations) or a realistic quality, informed by natural speech patterns.

Director Peter Hall, one of the most respected directors of Shakespeare in the past fifty years, explains this debate:

> I have worked in a theatre where the director before me urged the actors to run on from one line to the next, speak the text like prose. And to take breaths whenever they felt like it. He wanted them, he said, to be 'real'. They were; but they weren't comprehensible. I then arrived and said the opposite – that the line structure was the main instrument of communication. Its five beats make up a phrase which was by and large as much as an audience could take in without a sense break.
>
> (2003: 11)

Ultimately, the performance of Shakespeare's verse is a matter of balance, and, of course, personal choice.

In this section, we will look at elements of the verse structure that can help an actor in their delivery and highlight ways in which Shakespeare's verse form might relate to the meaning of the lines. We will also explore the areas of debate and disagreement.

The iambic pentameter

Exercise 1 – Clapping the line

These lines of pentameter are regular in their stress pattern (note the accent on the e of crownèd, which indicates that the ed ending needs to be pronounced as a separate syllable):

ORLANDO
    Hang there, my verse, in witness of my love.
    And thou, thrice-crownèd queen of night, survey

> With thy chaste eye, from thy pale sphere above,
> Thy huntress' name that my full life doth sway.
>
> (3.2.1–4)

- Speak these lines aloud whilst clapping the iambic pentameter rhythm.
- You should clap lightly on the unstressed syllable and heavily on the stressed syllable.

This exercise helps you to get a strong sense of what a regular line of pentameter sounds like. You could also try tapping the rhythm out on your chest, like a heartbeat.

Exercise 2 – Inventing lines of pentameter

In *The Actor and the Target,* Declan Donnellan suggests that a particularly good exercise for actors to become accustomed to the metre of Shakespeare's verse is to invent lines of iambic pentameter (2005: 285). The more that you speak in iambic pentameter, the more natural the rhythm will become to you. Although Dustin Hoffman famously said of Shakespeare's verse 'You can't improvise this shit' (Hall, 2003: 17), this isn't entirely true. Many actors, at least those accustomed to performing Shakespeare regularly, find that when forgetting their lines for a moment they manage to improvise in iambic pentameter.

Try making up your own lines of pentameter, clapping or beating your heart. This is not as difficult as it sounds. As George T. Wright states, 'Iambic pentameter has often been called the most speechlike of English meters, and this is undoubtedly true, especially of its blank verse form' (1988: 1). Here are a few examples:

> I think I'll go and have a cup of tea.
> I'm tired today, I need to have a rest.

- Have a go at making up some lines of your own.

Irregular verse

As was discussed in Chapter 2, there are a number of variations to the regular iambic pentameter. Practitioners often talk about these as indicative of the mood or feeling of a speech. Cicely Berry maintains that 'when the rhythm jumps or breaks in any way it means there is something dramatic happening, either within the action of the play or with the feeling and behaviour of the character . . . when the rhythm breaks within the text it does so because the character, to a large or small degree, is at odds with his natural rhythm' (1987: 53). This is a fairly broad claim, and, particularly in Shakespeare's later work where the metre becomes more changeable, looking for a reason for every rhythmic variation may be futile. However, it is useful to recognize where other metrical feet are substituted for an iamb, or where lines are metrically short or long and to consider whether this impacts in any way on your sense of a character's mood or intentions.

In Chapter 2 we looked at feminine endings and their possible functions of making dialogue 'speechlike', 'yearning' or 'questioning'. We also looked at anapaests, which can simply serve to make speech more conversational or can indicate a character's need for copious speech. And we looked at trochees and spondees which can sometimes provide forceful beginnings to speeches or lines.

Exercise 3 – Scanning the verse

Take the following speech and speak each line slowly, clapping or beating a regular pentameter:

ROSALIND
    And why, I pray you? Who might be your mother,
    That you insult, exult, and all at once
    Over the wretched? What though you have no beauty –
    As by my faith I see no more in you
    Than without candle may go dark to bed –
    Must you be therefore proud and pitiless?

(3.5.36–41)

- When you get to the end of the line, ask yourself 'Did that scan comfortably or were there words or syllables that seemed to get the wrong stress?'
- Go back over any section that didn't scan regularly and work out how the line scans most effectively (this is sometimes subjective and depends on how you choose to stress certain words).
- Is there a feminine ending, an anapaest, a trochee, a spondee or so on?
- Now ask yourself what you think might be the effect of the metrical variation (remembering, of course, that no particular effect is also a perfectly reasonable conclusion).

My own reading of the speech is as follows:

```
                                                Feminine ending
       u /    u/   u   /   u   /   u  /  u
    And why, I pray you? Who might be your mother
       u  /   /  u / u   u   /   u /           insult – trochee,
    That you insult, exult, and all at once    exult – trochee
    /  u  u  /  u   /     u   u   /   u /  u
    Over the wretched? What though you have no beauty
                                                Feminine ending;
                                                Over – trochee
                                                though you have
                                                – anapaest
                                                (although the
                                                anapaest could
                                                equally be '-ched?
                                                What though')
    u /  u   /   u/   u   /    u  /
    As by my faith I see no more in you
     /   u    /  /   u    /   u  /  u /
    Than without candle may go dark to bed –    Than with- –
                                                trochee-
                                                out can- –
                                                spondee
    /    u  u /  u   /    u   /  u /
    Must you be therefore proud and pitiless?   Must you –
                                                trochee
```

Line endings

As I discuss in *Shakespearean Verse Speaking,* there are two main opposing theories regarding the function of line endings in Shakespeare's verse. The first is that the verse structure provides the phrasing, taking precedence over the syntactical structure, and that the actor should breathe, pause or create a suspension at the end of each verse line. The most famous advocate of this method of delivery was Peter Hall. Hall believed entirely in the 'sanctity of the line' (2003: 24), maintaining that 'the end of each line is in fact a punctuation often more crucial that then regular punctuation itself' (2003: 28). On this basis he asserts that 'breaths whether small or substantial should only be taken at the end of the line' (2003: 29).

The second theory is that the grammatical sense takes precedence over the verse line in terms of phrasing and speech, and that the actor should breathe according to the punctuation. This is advocated by voice practitioner Patsy Rodenburg and director Declan Donnellan, amongst others. In contrast to Hall, Rodenburg criticizes the 'tendency to stop at the end of a line regardless of whether the end of the thought has been reached', asserting that that the actor should phrase with the thought as opposed to the verse. Donnellan asserts that 'if the verse and the sense are in conflict, then the actor is obliged to follow the sense' (2005: 283).

There is little evidence to support either method of delivery on the Renaissance stage, except for the fact that if the verse structure is ignored entirely then it differs little from prose, and there is a clear distinction in the way that the two mediums are used. There is also some evidence in George Puttenham's *The Art of English Poesie,* where Puttenham compares the marks of punctuation to the stops made by 'common travellers by the highways', whereby a comma represents 'a horseback calling perchance for a cup of beer or wine'; a colon the time when 'about noon he commeth to his Inn, & there baites himself and his horse an hour or more', and a full-stop, the time 'at night when he can conveniently travel no further'. He also asserts that 'our Poet when he hath made one verse, [i.e. one line of verse] hath as it were finished one day's journey' (1589: Book 2, Ch.4, 61–2), suggesting that the end of the verse line shares a function similar to a full-stop.

In Shakespeare's early work, line ending and phrase ending frequently coincide. This is called 'end-stopping'. However, there is a marked increase in enjambment in the process of Shakespeare's writing career with the sense running more frequently across the ends of lines. This is where the question of whether to phrase according to punctuation or line endings becomes most pertinent. Berry and Rodenburg both suggest exercises which encourage the actor to phrase according to the punctuation of a speech. Although the punctuation of a modern text is unlikely to represent that of the author it nevertheless often gives us a guide as to the general phrasing of a speech, and, as Berry argues, as to 'how the thoughts are cut up' (1987: 107). When characters are calm there are often few internal breaks within a line. However, when they are agitated there are often multiple breaks. A common exercise designed to help actors to find the grammatical phrasing of a speech is that of 'punctuation turns', where the actor is encouraged to walk their speech, changing direction on each strong phrase break.

Exercise 4 – Phrasing according to punctuation

We will look first at Duke Frederick's speech in 3.1:

DUKE FREDERICK
Not see him since? Sir, sir, that cannot be.
But were I not the better part made mercy
I should not seek an absent argument
Of my revenge, thou present. But look to it!
Find out thy brother wheresoe'er he is;
Seek him with candle. Bring him dead or living
Within this twelvemonth, or turn thou no more
To seek a living in our territory.
(3.1.1–8)

- Speak this speech aloud whilst walking.
- When you reach a mark of punctuation stronger than a comma (a semi-colon or a colon) take a quarter-turn.
- When you reach a full-stop, exclamation mark or question mark, take a half turn (180 degrees).

Now we will look at Jaques de Boys's speech in the final scene of the play. Repeat the exercise with this speech.

JAQUES DE BOYS
Let me have audience for a word or two.
I am the second son of old Sir Rowland,
That bring these tidings to this fair assembly.
Duke Frederick, hearing how that every day
Men of great worth resorted to this forest,
Address'd a mighty power, which were on foot,
In his own conduct, purposely to take
His brother here and put him to the sword;
And to the skirts of this wild wood he came,
Where meeting with an old religious man,
After some question with him, was converted
Both from his enterprise and from the world,
His crown bequeathing to his banish'd brother,
And all their lands restored to them again
That were with him exiled. This to be true,
I do engage my life.

(5.4.149–64)

This exercise provides you with a physical sense of the phrase-lengths in the speech. What I hope you will notice is that in the first speech, where Duke Frederick is agitated and delivering brusque orders, the phrases are short and staccato, whereas in the second speech, where Jaques de Boys is delivering urgent news about the duke's conversion, the phrases are much longer.

Exercise 5 – Phrasing according to the line ending

Now, we are going to read the two speeches above according to the method of only breathing at the end of verse lines.

- Read the first speech phrasing according to the line endings disregarding all internal punctuation.

What you might notice with the first speech is how this delivery forces you to begin one order immediately after another: 'Of my revenge, thou present. But look to it!' It is as if the duke does not want to pause for breath between his commands. This has been referred to as a 'Radio 4' moment – where a speaker doesn't want to pause for breath at the end of a sentence in case they are interrupted (much like interviewees on the *Today* programme).

– Now read the second speech phrasing according to the same method.

You may notice that this method slows you down in the second speech since the middle section is one long sentence: 'Duke Frederick . . . exiled'. You may also notice that when you insert a breath or brief suspension at the end of a line it naturally throws the emphasis onto the first strong syllable of the next line, particularly when the hesitation is ungrammatical. There are a few notable examples in this speech:

> Duke Frederick, hearing how that every day
> Men of great worth resorted to this forest,

Here the emphasis is thrown onto the word 'Men' which is an accented syllable at the start of the line. Jaques de Boys might pause briefly as he acknowledges those about whom he is speaking. A similar example comes a few lines later, where the emphasis is thrown onto an acknowledgement of Duke Senior:

> In his own conduct, purposely to take
> His brother here and put him to the sword;

In the following example, the line ending might give Jaques de Boys an opportunity to insert a rhetorical pause prior to his delivery of the climax of his news: the conversion of Duke Frederick. The emphasis is thrown onto the accented word 'Both':

> After some question with him, was converted
> Both from his enterprise and from the world,
>
> (5.4.159–60)

The purpose of this exercise is to investigate the effect of these different readings on characterisation. It is important to stress that an exclusive adherence to either method is reductive. The consistent observation of line endings with a pause has a tendency to become monotonous; however, in places, an ungrammatical pause created by a line ending might prove a useful tool of delivery.

Short verse lines

Short verse lines are lines that are less than five feet in length. The most common assertion about short lines in Shakespeare is that they imply a pause in the dialogue roughly equivalent to the number of missing syllables. Indeed, this theory is put forward by Hall, Barton, Berry, Rodenburg and a number of editors. According to Peter Hall, 'If a pause is wanted, Shakespeare leaves the pentameter incomplete. The silence is written as surely as it is in Pinter' (2000: 54–5). The rehearsal diaries for Sam Mendes' production of *King Lear* at the National Theatre, London in 2014 (written by staff director Tim Hoare) read as follows:

> During all of this, Sam has an eye on the verse, which always has clues about how Shakespeare is trying to direct his own play. When a character is speaking verse, but speaks in only a half-line (that is, anything less than the five beats of iambic pentameter), it is a good bet that Will is telling you to take a little pause for the rest of line (you observe the missing beats silently – unless someone's next words seem to perfectly complete an iambic line).
>
> (National Theatre Learning, 2014: 9)

This notion about short lines demanding a pause is one that I challenge both in relation to evidence from Elizabethan theatre practice and the context of such lines. In my view, some distinction must be drawn between different types of short line – those that begin a speech or end a speech, single half lines and those internal to a speech – since only those short lines internal to a speech would have been visible to actors working from a cue part. Elizabethan actors worked from parts containing their own lines and only a brief cue (two or three words). So, a part for Orlando for the beginning of 2.3, would have looked something like this:

-------------------------- bears it!

ORLANDO   Why, what's the matter?
------------------------------ enter it!

ORLANDO   Why whither Adam, wouldst thou have me go?
------------------------------ not here.

ORLANDO   What, wouldst thou have me go and beg my food

It would have been impossible for the actor, faced with only two or three words of the preceding line to discern the metrical connection of their lines to those of other characters, since they would not be able to distinguish a short cue-line from a full cue-line. Orlando has no means of telling that 'bears it!' is the end of a short, seven-syllable line, whereas 'enter it!' is the end of a full ten-syllable line. As a result, I am doubtful that actors working from parts would have perceived short verse lines as indicative of a pause, with the exception of those internal to speeches (for more on this see Rokison, 2011). It is possible that the actor might have recognized these distinctions once he began to perform the scene. However, the work of Tiffany Stern and others has shown us that Renaissance actors had limited rehearsal time, and probably committed their roles to memory before they began acting with the other actors, invariably making interpretative decisions in the process.

My contention is that short lines, other than those internal to speeches, do not function as pauses, and I think that in many cases the context of the lines backs up the evidence from cue parts.

Exercise 6 – Single and final short lines – testing the effect

Here is a selection of passages from *As You Like It* that contain short verse lines (the short lines are in bold):

ROSALIND
    Then good my liege, mistake me not so much
    To think my poverty is treacherous.
CELIA
    Dear sovereign, hear me speak.
DUKE FREDERICK
    Ay, Celia, we stayed her for your sake,

                                                         (1.3.61–4)

DUKE SENIOR
    Why, how now, Monsieur! What a life is this
    That your poor friends must woo your company!
    What, you look merrily.
JAQUES
    A fool, a fool! I met a fool i'th' forest,

                                                         (2.7.9–12)

JAQUES
    A worthy fool! Motley's the only wear!
DUKE SENIOR
    What fool is this?
JAQUES
    O worthy fool! – One that hath been a courtier,

                                                         (2.7.34–6)

ROSALIND
    She has a housewife's hand – but that's no matter.
    I say she never did invent this letter;
    This is a man's invention and his hand.
SILVIUS
    Sure it is hers.

ROSALIND
   Why, 'tis a boisterous and a cruel style,

                                                           (4.3.27–31)

- Read one or more of the passages in groups of two or three inserting a pause roughly equivalent to the number of missing syllables after the short line. Discuss the effect of this on the sense and mood of the exchange.
- Now read the same passage or passages with all speakers coming in on cue. Again, discuss the effect.

Once again, there is no right or wrong answer, and different people might prefer different readings. I would argue that in the case of all these passages it makes more dramatic sense for the readers to come in on cue. The effect might be one of rapid interjection, interruption, or even, in the case of the final example, overlap. Rosalind might continue her invective against Phoebe, barely pausing to acknowledge Silvius's comment. Such a mode of delivery could have been indicated to Renaissance actors by giving the actor playing Rosalind a continuous speech and the actor playing Silvius the cue 'his hand'.

Single short lines in Shakespeare's plays are often composed of succinct questions, answers, imperatives, exclamations, interjections and confirmations and the succeeding lines often begin with words like 'Ay', 'O', 'Why' or other exclamations that seem to benefit from an immediate response.

Shared verse lines

In a number of cases, when one speaker delivers a short verse line the next speaker metrically completes it:

ORLANDO
   Why, what's the matter?
ADAM   O, unhappy youth,

                                                              (2.3.16)

In most cases the connection between such lines is uncontroversial, and editions indent the second portion of the line in order to make visually explicit the connection. The most common assertion about shared verse lines, made by theatre practitioners, is that the second actor should come in on cue without leaving a break, making a metrical whole of the two halves. This seems to make sense. It is reasonable to assume that actors who had only their cue to rely on, might have entered fairly promptly when hearing their cue-words spoken.

It is also commonly asserted that shared verse lines (lines of verse divided between two characters) are indicative of conflict. There is a precedent for the use of stichomythia (alternating half-line exchanges) for violent disputation in classical Roman drama and in Tudor plays. Some passages in Shakespeare seem similarly constructed, especially when a shared line is made up of more than two parts:

> DUKE FREDERICK
> Mistress, dispatch you with your safest haste
> And get you from our court.
> ROSALIND   Me, uncle?
> DUKE FREDERICK   You, cousin.
>
> (1.3.38–9)

You might look out for such ways in which the structure of the verse enhances the tone of the dialogue. However, there is a danger of generalisation about shared lines – that they are invariably indicative of hasty dialogue in which the second speaker interrupts the first. This might not always be the case, and is dependent on the period of composition, the context of the passage and the structure of the scene.

Exercise 7 – Shared lines

- Read these two different passages that include shared lines.
- Experiment with coming in on cue with every line.
- What is the effect of one speaker finishing the metre of another's line? Is the effect different depending on the passage?

Passage 1

DUKE FREDERICK
    Mistress, dispatch you with your safest haste
    And get you from our court.
ROSALIND   Me, uncle?
DUKE FREDERICK   You, cousin.
    Within these ten days if that thou be'est found
    So near our public court as twenty miles,
    Thou diest for it.
ROSALIND   I do beseech your grace,
    Let me the knowledge of my fault bear with me.
    If with myself I hold intelligence,
    Or have acquaintance with mine own desires,
    If that I do not dream, or be not frantic –
    As I do trust I am not – then, dear uncle,
    Never so much as in a thought unborn
    Did I offend your highness.
DUKE FREDERICK   Thus do all traitors.

                                                  (1.3.38–49)

Passage 2

CORIN
    Mistress and master, you have oft enquired
    After the shepherd that complained of love,
    Who you saw sitting by me on the turf,
    Praising the proud disdainful shepherdess
    That was his mistress.
CELIA   Well, and what of him?
CORIN
    If you will see a pageant truly played
    Between the pale complexion of true love
    And the red glow of scorn and proud disdain,
    Go hence a little and I shall conduct you,
    If you will mark it.
ROSALIND   O come, let us remove –
    The sight of lovers feedeth those in love.

                                                  (3.4.43–52)

Three consecutive shared lines

There are moments in Shakespeare's plays where the question of linking short lines becomes vexed. This is most often the case where the text contains three consecutive short lines, either pair of which could be linked to form a pentameter line:

> ADAM
>   Envenoms him that bears it!
> ORLANDO
>   Why, what's the matter?
> ADAM
>   O unhappy youth,

The Arden Third Edition prints these lines as follows:

> ADAM [. . .]
>   Envenoms him that bears it!
> ORLANDO
>   Why, what's the matter?
> ADAM   O unhappy youth,
>   Come not within these doors! Within this roof
>   The enemy of all your graces lives.
>
>   (2.3.15–18)

This seems to imply that the first of the lines is a short line, and the second and third a shared verse line. This is not particularly problematic, except for an actor taught to regard a short line as indicating a pause and a shared line as indicating a swift intervention.

The lines could equally be printed:

> ADAM
>   Envenoms him that bears it!
> ORLANDO   Why, what's the matter?
> ADAM
>   O unhappy youth,
>   Come not within these doors! Within this roof
>   The enemy of all your graces lives.

The first two lines can form a shared line should 'it! / Why what's' be regarded as an anapaest.

For similar reasons to the perceived function of short verse lines, I would argue that a Renaissance actor would have been unable to see such a metrical structure and is thus likely to have come in more or less on cue with each line.

Exercise 8 – Three consecutive shared lines

- Try reading this passage with both actors coming in on cue with each speech.

    ADAM
       Envenoms him that bears it!
    ORLANDO
       Why, what's the matter?
    ADAM
       O unhappy youth,

- What is the effect?

Examples of three consecutive short lines often come in passages of increased tension and may provide a sort of enhanced version of the effect of a shared line, providing an increase in pace in the dialogue.

Performing rhetoric

In Chapter 2 we explored the use of rhetoric in *As You Like It*, looking in detail at rhetorical tropes and figures used by various characters.

Assonance and alliteration

Two of the most common rhetorical devices found in Shakespeare's writing are assonance and alliteration. The sound of a speech often relates closely to its subject matter. Those known as plosive consonants because they explode on the lips (such as *p*, *b*, *t* and *d*) and the fricatives (such as *f* and *v*) and the hard *c* sound are often indicative of anger or aggression, whilst soft consonants (*l*, *m*, *n*) are often found in gentler, more fluid dialogue. This, of course, depends on the context. An *s* can sound like hissing or spitting, or it can sound soft and caressing, depending on how it is voiced. With vowels, long vowel sounds such as *ee* (iː), *ah* (aː), *oo* (uː), *or* (ɔː) and *er* (ɜː) and diphthongs (sounds made up of two vowels) – *ay* (eɪ), *eye* (aɪ), *oy* (ɔɪ) *ow* (aʊ) *oh* (əʊ) and *air* (eə) are often indicative of an outpouring of emotion, coming from straight the diaphragm. Short vowels, such as *a* (æ), *e* (e), *i* (ɪ), *o* (ɒ) and *u* (ʌ) are often characteristic of more matter of fact or vicious utterances.

John Barton asserts that modern actors have a tendency 'to run away from verbal relish, especially of vowels' but also of consonants (1984: 54). Cicely Berry suggests that the actor needs to gain an awareness of 'the length and movement of the vowels and the length and vibration of the consonants' (1987: 29). These next two exercises are often used by actors to find the connection between the language and the emotional quality of a speech. I see it as a form of practical exploration of assonance and alliteration. By speaking the words aloud, we are able to hear sounds patterns that might not be immediately obvious on the page.

Exercise 1 – Isolating vowels

We are going to take two speeches from *As You Like It*. The first is Orlando's speech in 3.2, as he hangs his love poems on the trees:

ORLANDO
    Hang there, my verse, in witness of my love
    And thou, thrice-crowned queen of night, survey
    With thy chaste eye, from thy pale sphere above,
    Thy huntress' name that my full life doth sway.

> O Rosalind, these trees shall be my books,
> And in their barks my thoughts I'll character,
> That every eye which in this forest looks
> Shall see thy virtue witnessed everywhere.
> Run, run Orlando, carve on every tree
> The fair, the chaste and unexpressive she!
>
> (3.2.1–10)

The second is Phoebe's speech to Silvius at the start of 3.5:

> PHOEBE
> I would not be thy executioner;
> I fly thee for I would not injure thee.
> Thou tell'st me there is murder in mine eye.
> 'Tis pretty, sure, and very probable
> That eyes, that are the frail'st and softest things,
> Who shut their coward gates on atomies,
> Should be called tyrants, butchers, murderers.
>
> (3.5.8–14)

- Try to speak these speeches verbalizing only the vowel sounds, for example, the start of Orlando's speech would sound something like this:

  a ore eye er, i i-e o eye u
  a ow, eye-ow-e ee o eye er-ey

- Concentrate on feeling the length of the long vowels and diphthongs.
- Notice sounds that are regularly repeated. Some may surprise you.
- Try to connect physically with the vowel sounds.
- How do you feel as you speak each speech?
- What are the differences between the two speeches?

Orlando's speech contains quite a lot of long, open vowel sounds – air, eye, ow, ey. Note the open 'O' at the start of line 5. An *O* is an open expression of emotion or 'emotional release' (Barton, 1984:142). Actors are sometimes embarrassed by these. Try to use the full length of the *O* to express Orlando's passion for Rosalind.

Phoebe's speech contains more short vowel sounds in quick succession, in words like 'executioner' and 'probable'. But we should also notice the long vowel sounds with which many of the lines begin.

Exercise 2 – Stressing the consonants

As Cicely Berry states, 'The same exercise can be done with consonants', but this is far more difficult (1987: 152). Easier is to exaggerate the consonant sounds in a reading of a speech, so that you feel them in your mouth, and notice the repetition of sounds.

- Using the same two speeches above, speak each speech exaggerating the consonant sounds.
- Again, notice the presence of repeated sounds (which may not look alike on the page).
- Again, try to connect with the sounds, thinking about how different vowel sounds can be articulated.

We might notice that Orlando's speech contains a high proportion of soft consonants: *h, m, v, s, w, l*. Phoebe's speech contains more plosives and harsh fricatives: *f, t, p, b, c*. Take line 14, for example. You can imagine Phoebe spitting the *sh, b, c, t, b* sounds at the beginning of consecutive words.

Imagery

Shakespeare's use of imagery, including metaphor, simile, personification and metonymy, can be complex. His use of word order is also sometimes surprising to the modern speaker. A useful exercise with which to explore the complexity and richness of the language is to try to put it into your own words. This not only ensures that you understand what you are saying but can draw attention to the words that the character chooses to use.

Exercise 3 – Putting it into your own words

Let us take Silvius's lines in 3.5 as an example:

SILVIUS
    Sweet Phoebe, do not scorn me, do not Phoebe.
    Say that you love me not, but say not so
    In bitterness. The common executioner,
    Whose heart, th'accustomed sight of death makes hard,
    Falls not the axe upon the humbled neck
    But first begs pardon. Will you sterner be
    Than he that dies and lives by bloody drops?
    . . .

SILVIUS
    O dear Phoebe,
    If ever – as that ever may be near –
    You meet in some fresh cheek the power of fancy,
    Then shall you know the wounds invisible
    That love's keen arrows make.

                                                    (3.5.1–32)

- Try to put Silvius's lines into your own words.
- Don't worry if this takes some time.
- Also, don't worry about elegance of expression; you are trying to unpick Shakespeare's language, not create your own verse.

Exercise 4 – 'Attending to the word'

Cicely Berry describes sitting in on a rehearsal of Peter Brook's *Antony and Cleopatra,* from which she got this exercise, 'attending to the word' (1987: 157–8). Having explored the speeches in your own words, you are now going to attend very closely to the words used by Shakespeare.

- Speak the speeches aloud, paying attention to every single word that you speak.
- Berry asserts that you must 'really feel the energy and texture of each word complete and fulfilled before you allow yourself to go on to the next' (Berry, 1987: 158).

In doing this exercise you should gain a keen sense of how the words relate to one another; how they are ordered; which words stand out.

Exercise 5 – Physicalizing words and images

In this exercise you are going to physically explore the words in the text. This exercise is particularly helpful in ensuring that words are imbued with meaning, and not just spoken. When we tell someone else something, we have a mental image of the thing about which we are speaking – be it a loved one, something terrifying or something funny – not only in our minds but also in our bodies, a physical sensation connected to the experience. It is those elements that help to colour the way in which we relate a story. In order to give the words of a character a similar veracity, it can be helpful to gain both a mental image and a physical sensation of whatever they are articulating.

- Take Silvius's first speech (above). Go through the speech slowly, looking for the key words, for example, 'Sweet', 'scorn', 'love', 'bitterness', 'executioner', 'heart', 'death', 'hard' etc.
- As you come to each word, try to get a mental image of it.
- Try physicalizing the word, giving it an action, which helps to express it.
- Exaggerate the physicalization, whilst speaking the word aloud.
- Gradually reduce the size of the physical image and the volume of our speech.
- Now try speaking the word again. See if you feel more connected to it.

- Once you have done this exercise for each of the key words, try putting the speech back together again.

One of the dangers of this exercise is that individual words can become over-emphasized. Try to speak as fluently and naturally as possible, whilst letting the images that you created come to mind.

Antithesis

Antithesis is another important rhetorical device. Many leading directors of Shakespeare speak of antithesis as one of the most important structures to grasp in a delivery of the Shakespearean text. In a tribute to John Barton, Gregory Doran cites 'go for the antithesis' as one of the factors that he and Barton considered most important in helping an actor to 'make the audience listen' (2018). Patsy Rodenburg warns that 'many of Shakespeare's speeches require the actor to recognise the intellectual power of antithesis. The actor who fails to see and explore it in the moment of speaking will flatten the complexity of thought and debate and fail to travel the journey of the speech' (2002: 122).

Exercise 6 – Tapping the antithesis

Certainly it is important for an actor to identify the instances of antithesis in their lines. Berry suggests that when reading a speech through an actor should tap their hand 'on something on all the antithetical words' (1987: 91).

- Read the following speech, tapping you hand on each instance of antithesis.

   PHOEBE
   Think not I love him though I ask for him:
   'Tis but a peevish boy – yet he talks well;
   But what care I for words? yet words do well

When he that speaks them pleases those that hear.
It is a pretty youth – not very pretty –
But sure he's proud, and yet his pride becomes him.
He'll make a proper man. The best thing in him
Is his complexion; and faster than his tongue
Did make offence his eye did heal it up.
He is not very tall; yet for his years he's tall;
His leg is but so-so, and yet 'tis well.
There was a pretty redness in his lip,
A little riper and more lusty red
Than that mixed in his cheek. 'Twas just the difference
Between the constant red and mingled damask.
There be some women, Silvius, had they marked him
In parcels as I did, would have gone near
To fall in love with him; but for my part
I love him not – nor hate him not. And yet
I have more cause to hate him than to love him,
For what had he to do to chide at me?
He said mine eyes were black and my hair black,
And, now I am remembered, scorned at me.
I marvel why I answered not again.
But that's all one – omittance is no quittance.
I'll write to him a very taunting letter
And thou shalt bear it. Wilt thou, Silvius?

(3.5.110–36)

- Now take a pen and underline all the antithetical words or phrases.

This whole speech is built around a tension between what Phoebe really feels and what she is pretending to feel. In exploring this tension, Phoebe uses a number of antithetical words and phrases; some contained within a single verse line (speaks . . . hear; love . . . hate; hate . . . love), some stretching across the lines (tongue . . . eye).

Exercise 7 – Physicalizing the antithesis

- As you speak the speech aloud this time you are going to physicalize the pull that exists between two antithetical ideas or images, by moving from side to side – one way on the first image and the other way on the second.
- Recalling what you did in Exercise 5, take each example of antithesis and try physicalizing the two opposing ideas, one after the other, moving from one side to the other as you do this.
- Start quite big and then gradually reduce the physicality until you are just speaking the two words or phrases again, whilst stepping to the side, and finally just standing still, weighing the two words or images in your hands.

Other figures of balance and repetition

As well as the figure of antithesis, Phoebe uses a number of other rhetorical figures of balance and repetition in this speech as she sets out the two sides of her debate.

Exercise 8 – Marking the repetition

- Take a pen of another colour from that with which you have marked the antithesis.
- Remind yourself of the other key figures of repetition that we explored when discussing rhetoric: anaphora, epistrophe, anadiplosis, chiasmus etc.
- Read through the speech, marking any figures of repetition. For example: 'But what care I for words? Yet words do well' (anadiplosis); 'He is not very tall; yet for his years he's tall' (epistrophe); 'I love him not – not hate him not. And yet / I have more cause to hate him than to love him' (chiasmus).

Exercise 9 – Physicalizing the debate

Finally, having marked all the rhetorical figures we are going to use them to physicalize Phoebe's argument, to which there are clearly two sides – don't think that I love him . . . except I do. It is useful to clarify the sense of back and forth that is happening in the speech. This can be done physically.

- Imagine that Ganymede is standing on the opposite side of the room.
- Every time your argument expresses a feeling of love towards Ganymede, take a step towards the imaginary figure.
- Every time your argument denies that love, take a step away.
- This exercise should help you to find the abrupt changes that take place in the speech.
- You might also notice how balanced the phrases are, with the mid-line caesura often providing the moment of change:

    - Think not I love him   though I ask for him
    - Tis but a peevish boy   yet he talks well
    - It is a pretty youth   not very pretty
    - But sure he's proud   and yet his pride becomes him

Performing 'you' and 'thou'

Finally, we are going to look at the terms of address 'you' and 'thou' and their constituent parts. As was discussed in Chapter 2, the personal pronouns used by characters are significant in what they reveal about their relationships to others and the changes that occur in those relationships. We noted that 'you' is the more formal pronoun, whilst 'thou' is used more intimately or aggressively. The two seemingly opposing functions of 'thou' provide the actor with some interesting choices.

Exercise 1 – Exploring 'you' and 'thou'.

This is a useful exercise to do with any scene in which any of the characters use a mixture of personal pronouns. We are going to look at the beginning of 1.3 and the role of Celia (lines 1–32).

- Go through the text underlining in one colour the instances when Celia uses 'you' or 'your' and in another colour the moments when she uses 'thou' or 'thee' or 'thy'.
- Celia begins by using 'thy' to Rosalind – 'No, thy words are too precious to be cast away upon curs' (ll.4–5). Consider whether Celia is using the 'thou' form in an affectionate or aggressive manner. This is not particularly difficult here; Celia is clearly trying to get Rosalind to confide in her.
- The next time that Celia speaks, however, she uses 'your' – 'But is all this for your father?' Why might she have changed in her use of pronoun? Is there something less intimate or more reserved about this question?
- Now look at the pattern of usage and, in particular, at any changes in terms of address through the rest of this passage. Consider why Celia might change her use of pronoun towards Rosalind and what this might indicate about the tone of a line and the warmth or distance in their relationship at any one moment.
- If you are working in pairs, try putting the scene on its feet. Experiment with ways in which the use of different pronouns might dictate the physicality of the relationship.

Exercise 2 – What sort of 'thou'?

Given that thou is the less common form of address and the form that can be most ambiguous in its usage, it is always worth exploring the type of 'thou' one character uses to another. We are going to continue with 1.3, but now we are going to look at the role of Duke Frederick.

- Underline the personal pronouns used by Duke Frederick between lines 38–86, using one colour for 'you' and its constituent parts and one for 'thou' and its constituent parts.
- Frederick begins by using 'you' to Rosalind. This is the formal term of address, so might suggest something about how the line is played.
- At line 40 he shifts abruptly to 'thou'. Decide what sort of 'thou' is being played here.
- When Celia intervenes, Frederick first addresses her with 'your' (line 64). This is perhaps unusual given that she is his daughter. It might indicate a certain resumption of formality, or a deliberate distancing.
- At line 74, as with his dialogue with Rosalind, he shifts to 'thou'. Is this the same sort of 'thou' as that used towards Rosalind? Frederick might be losing his temper with Celia or you could try a deliberately patronising tone, or a smothering one in which he attempts to show his daughter how much more special she is than Rosalind. Try all of these options.
- Finally, Frederick moves again to 'you' for both Rosalind and Celia. What does this say about the tone of his parting lines?
- Again, try putting the scene on its feet and exploring the physicality of these choices. Might Frederick touch either Rosalind or Celia at any point in the scene? What sort of contact might this be? Might he move towards or away from either of them at any point?
- Use the changes in pronoun to guide your choices.

Writing matters

Metre in performance

Choose a passage from the play and consider how the metrical structure might influence its delivery in performance.

Line endings in performance

Choose a passage and make an argument for phrasing it either according to the line endings or the verse structure.

Exploring language physically

Why might it be useful to explore language physically, rather than solely on the page?

BIBLIOGRAPHY

Editions

Brissenden, Alan, ed. (1993), *As You Like It,* Oxford: Oxford University Press.
Capell, Edward, ed. (1767–8), *Mr. William Shakespeare, his comedies, histories, and tragedies,* London.
Dusinberre, Juliet, ed. (2006), *As You Like It,* London: The Arden Shakespeare.
Furness, H. H., ed. (1890), *As You Like It,* Philadelphia: New Variorum Edition.
Greenblatt, Stephen, Walter Cohen, and Jean E. Howard, eds (1997) *The Norton Shakespeare,* New York: W W Norton & Company.
Latham, Agnes, ed. (1975), *As You Like It,* London: Methuen.

Films

As You Like It (2006), [Film] Dir. Kenneth Branagh, UK/ USA: BBC Films/ HBO.
As You Like It (1992), [Film] Dir. Christine Edzard, UK: Sands Films.

Other sources

Astington, John H. (1999), *English Court Theatre, 1558–1642,* Cambridge: Cambridge University Press.
Baggot, Emma (2019), Interview with author.
Barber, C. L. (1959), *Shakespeare's Festive Comedies,* Princeton: Princeton University Press.
Barton, John (1984), *Playing Shakespeare,* London: Methuen.
Beckerman, Bernard (1962), *Shakespeare at the Globe,* New York: Macmillan.
Berry, Cicely (1987), *The Actor and his Text,* London: Harrap.

Block, Giles (2013), *Speaking the Speech*, London: Nick Hern.
Bradbrook, Muriel (1969), *Shakespeare the Craftsman,* London: Chatto & Windus.
Burke, K. (1950), *A Rhetoric of Motives,* New York: Prentice Hall.
Capell, Edward (1779), *Notes and Various Reading to Shakespeare*, Vol. 1, London.
Carroll, Tim (2008), 'Practising Behaviour to his Own Shadow', in Karim-Cooper, Farah and Carson, Christie (eds), 37–44, *Shakespeare's Globe: A Theatrical Experiment,* Cambridge: CUP.
Chambers, E. K. (1923), *The Elizabethan Stage,* Oxford: Clarendon Press.
Chiari, Sophie (2019), *Shakespeare's Representation of Weather, Climate and Environment,* Edinburgh: EUP.
Craig, Hugh and Brett Greatley-Hirsch (2017), *Style, Computers and Early Modern Drama: Beyond Authorship,* Cambridge: CUP.
Crystal, David (2002), 'To modernize or not to modernize: there is no question', *Around the Globe,* 21: 15–17.
Crystal, David (2016), *The Oxford Dictionary of Original Shakespearean Pronunciation,* Oxford: OUP.
Danson, Lawrence (2000), *Shakespeare's Dramatic Genres,* Oxford: OUP.
Dessen, Alan (1984), *Elizabethan Stage Conventions and Modern Interpreters,* Cambridge: CUP.
Dickson, Andrew (2015), 'As You Like It: "This was Shakespeare trying to write The Fast Show"', *Guardian,* 2 November.
DiGangi, Mario (1996), 'Queering the Shakespearean Family', *Shakespeare Quarterly,* 47, no. 3 (Autumn): 269–90.
Donnellan, Declan (2005), *The Actor and the Target*, Cambridge: MIT Press.
Doran, Gregory (2018), 'John Barton, RSC Artistic Director, Gregory Doran, reflects on the life of John Barton', available online: https://www.rsc.org.uk/about-us/history/key-past-people/john-barton (accessed 4 May 2020)
Dusinberre, Juliet (2003a), 'Topical Forest: Kemp and Mar-text in Arden', in Thompson, Ann and McMullan, Gordon (eds), *In Arden: Editing Shakespeare*, 239–51, London: Arden.
Dusinberre, Juliet (2003b), 'Pancakes and a Date for "As You like It"', *Shakespeare Quarterly*, 54, no. 4: 371–405
Egan, Gabriel (2001), 'The Globe Theatre' in Wells, Stanley and Dobson, Michael (eds), *The Oxford Companion to Shakespeare*, 165–6, Oxford: OUP.
Elam, Keir (1984), *Shakespeare's Universe of Discourse: Language-Games in the Comedies,* Cambridge: Cambridge University Press.
Escolme, Bridget (2004), *Talking to the Audience,* London: Routledge.

Euanthius, Giovanni Cupaiuolo (1974), '*De Fabula*' (trans. O. B Hardison Jr), in Preminger, Alex, Hardison Jr., O. B and Kerrane, Kevin (eds), *Classical and Medieval Literary Criticism*, New York: F. Ungar.
Freedman, Penelope (2007), *Power and Passion in Shakespeare's Pronouns*, Aldershot: Ashgate.
Frye, Roland Mushat (1982), *Shakespeare: The Art of the Dramatist*, London: Allen & Unwin.
Furness, Hannah (2015), 'William Shakespeare's jokes are just not funny, Richard Eyre admits', *Telegraph*, 23 June.
Garber, Margery (1986), 'The Education of Orlando', in Braunmuller, A.R., and Bulman, J. C., *Comedy from Shakespeare to Sheridan*, 102–12, Newark: University of Delaware Press.
Gurr, Andrew (1992), *The Shakespearean Stage, 1574–1642*, Cambridge: CUP.
Gurr, Andrew (2004), *The Shakespeare Company, 1594–1642*, Cambridge: CUP.
Gurr, Andrew (2011), '"The stage is hung with black": Genre and the Trappings of Stagecraft in Shakespearean Tragedy', in Guneratne, A.R. (ed.), *Shakespeare and Genre*, 67–82, New York: Palgrave Macmillan.
Hall, Peter (2000), *Exposed by the Mask*, London: Oberon.
Hall, Peter (2003), *Shakespeare's Advice to the Players*, London: Oberon.
Hanks, Robert (1996), 'Review of *As You Like It*', *Evening Standard*, 28 October.
Hardison, O.B., Jr. and Kerrane, Kevin, eds (1974), *Medieval Literary Criticism*, New York: Frederick Ungar Publishing.
Harmon, William, ed. (2005), *Classic Writings on Poetry*, New York: Columbia University Press.
Hirsch, James E. (2003), *Shakespeare and the History of Soliloquies*, Madison, NJ: Fairleigh Dickinson University Press.
Hodgdon, Barbara (2002), 'Sexual Disguise and the Theatre of Gender', in Leggatt, Alexander (ed.), *The Cambridge Companion to Shakespearean Comedy*, 179–97, Cambridge: CUP.
Hyland, Peter (2011), *Disguise on the Early Modern English Stage*, Farnham: Ashgate.
Hytner, Nicholas (2015), Interview with author.
Jackson, Russell (2000), 'From Playscript to Screenplay', in Jackson, Russell (ed.), *The Cambridge Companion to Shakespeare on Film*, 15–34, Cambridge: CUP.
Jourdain, W.C. (1860), 'Some proposed emendations in the text of Shakespeare and explanation of his words', in *Transactions of the Philological Society*, 133–44, London.
Lamb, Jonathan P. (2017), *Shakespeare in the Marketplace of Words*, Cambridge: CUP.

Leishman, James Blair (1949), *The Three Parnassus Plays (1598–1601)*, London: Nicholson & Watson.
Lodge, Thomas (1590), *Rosalynde. Euphues Golden Legacie*, London.
Lyly, John (1578), *Euphues. the Anatomy of vvyt Very Pleasant for all Gentlemen to Reade, and most Necessary to Remember*, London.
Lyly, John (1584), *Campaspe Played Beefore the Queenes Maiestie on Newyeares Day at Night, by Her Maiesties Childre[n], and the Children of Paules*, London.
Marx, Steven (2000), *Shakespeare and the Bible*, Oxford: OUP.
McDonald, Russ (2001), *Shakespeare and the Arts of Language*, Oxford: OUP.
Miola, Robert (2000), *Shakespeare's Reading*, Oxford: OUP.
National Theatre Learning (2014), *King Lear, Background Pack: Rehearsal Diaries*, available online: https://www.tes.com/teaching-resource/king-lear-background-pack-1-rehearsal-diaries-6396018 (accessed 29 April 2020)
Nordlund, Marcus (2017), *The Shakespearean Inside: A Study of the Complete Soliloquies and Solo Asides*, Edinburgh: Edinburgh University Press.
Potter, Lois (1990), '"Nobody's Perfect": Actors' Memories and Shakespeare's Plays of the 1590s', *Shakespeare Survey* 42: 85–98
Purcell, Stephen (2018), 'Are Shakespeare's plays always metatheatrical?', *Shakespeare Bulletin*, 36, no. 1: 19–35.
Puttenham, George (1589), *The Arte of English Poesie*, London.
Rhodes, Neil (2004), *Shakespeare and the Origins of English*, Oxford: OUP.
Richmond, Hugh Macrae (2002), *Shakespeare's Theatre: A Dictionary of his Stage Context*, London: Continuum.
Rodenburg, Patsy (2002), *Speaking Shakespeare*, London: Methuen.
Rokison, Abigail (2005), 'Shakespeare in Performance at the second biennial British Shakespeare Association conference at the University of Newcastle-upon-Tyne', *Shakespeare* 1, no. 1–2: 188–202.
Rokison, Abigail (2011), *Shakespearean Verse Speaking*, Cambridge: CUP.
Rokison-Woodall, Abigail (2017), *Shakespeare in the Theatre: Nicholas Hytner*, London: The Arden Shakespeare.
Rutter, Carol (1984) *Documents of the Rose Playhouse*, Manchester: MUP.
Shapiro, James (2015), 'Shakespeare in Modern English?', *New York Times*, 7 October.
Shapiro, Michael (1994), *Gender in Play on the Shakespearean Stage: Boy Heroines and Female Pages*, Ann Arbour: University of Michigan Press.
Sidney, Philip (1595), *The Defence of Poesie*, London.
Skinner, Quentin (2014), *Forensic Shakespeare*, Oxford: OUP.
Smallwood, Robert (2003), *Shakespeare at Stratford: As You Like It*, London: The Arden Shakespeare.

Stelling, Lieke (2019), *Religious Conversion in Early Modern English Drama*, Cambridge: CUP.
Stern, Tiffany (2004), *Making Shakespeare*, London: Routledge.
Stern, Tiffany (2009), *Documents of Performance in Early Modern England*, Cambridge: CUP.
Stern, Tiffany and Simon Palfrey (2007), *Shakespeare in Parts*, Oxford: OUP.
Tarlinskaja, Marina (2014), *Shakespeare and the Versification of English Drama, 1561–1642*, Farnham: Ashgate.
Taylor, Gary, ed. (1982), *Henry V*, Oxford: OUP.
Tennant, David (1998), 'Touchstone in *As You Like It*', in Smallwood, Robert (ed.), *Players of Shakespeare 4*, 30–44, Cambridge: CUP.
Thompson, Craig R., trans. (1978), '*De Ratione Studii*', in *The Collected works of Erasmus*, vol. XXIV, Toronto: University of Toronto Press.
Thorne, Alison (2000), *Vision and Rhetoric in Shakespeare: Looking Through Language*, Basingstoke: Macmillan.
Traub, Valerie (2001), 'The Homoerotics of Shakespearean Comedy', in Chedgzoy, Kate (ed.), *Shakespeare, Feminism and Gender*, 117–44, Hampshire: Palgrave.
Tripney, Natasha (2018), 'Hamlet, thy name is woman: Why Michelle Terry's Globe is staging post-gender Shakespeare', *Independent*, 14 May.
Tripney, Natasha (2019), 'Review of *As You Like It*', *The Stage*, 21 February.
van Es, Bart (2015), *Shakespeare in Company*, Oxford: OUP.
Vickers, Brian (1971), 'Shakespeare's Use of Rhetoric', in Muir, Kenneth and Schoenbaum, S. (eds), *A New Companion to Shakespeare Studies*, 85–101, Cambridge: CUP.
Vickers, Brian (1985), 'Shakespeare's Use of Prose', in Andrews, John F. (ed.), *William Shakespeare: His World, His Work, His Influence*, 389–95, New York: Scribner.
Warren, Roger (1986), 'Shakespeare in Britain, 1985', *Shakespeare Quarterly*, 37, no. 1: 114–20.
Weimann, Robert (1978), *Shakespeare and the Popular Tradition in the Theater: Studies in the Social Dimension of the Dramatic Form and Function*, London: John Hopkins University Press.
Wells, Stanley (1984), *Re-Editing Shakespeare for the Modern Reader*, Oxford: Clarendon Press.
Wiggins, Martin (2019), 'The Cast of Measure for Measure', lecture, University of Kent, 7 November.
Wiggins, Martin and Catherine Teresa Richardson (2014), *British Drama, 1533–1642: A Catalogue, Volume 4*, Oxford: OUP.
Wright, George T. (1988), *Shakespeare's Metrical Art*, Berkeley: University of California Press.

www.ingramcontent.com/pod-product-compliance
Ingram Content Group UK Ltd.
Pitfield, Milton Keynes, MK11 3LW, UK
UKHW030003161224
452559UK00010B/223